Ernest Lucas

Scripture Union
130 City Road, London EC1V 2NJ

First published 1989 by Scripture Union
130 City Road, London EC1V 2NJ

ISBN 0 86201 534 0

British Library Cataloguing in Publication Data
Lucas, Ernest
Genesis Today
1. Bible. O.T. Genesis—critical studies
I. Title
222′.1106
ISBN 0–86201–534–0

Designed by Sue Ainley
Phototypeset by Input Typesetting Ltd, London
Printed and bound by Cox & Wyman Ltd, Reading

Contents

Thanks

This book has been several years in the making. I want to express my thanks to all those who have helped me to write it.

It is impossible to mention everyone who helped me develop my thinking about science and Christianity in general, and science and Genesis in particular – by their lectures, books, letters and personal conversations. Many of these have been members of the The American Scientific Affiliation, Christians in Science (formerly The Research Scientists' Christian Fellowship), the Creation Research Society and The Tyndale Fellowship for Biblical Research. They, of course, are not to be held responsible for my conclusions. Some would certainly not accept particular ones.

Thanks are also due to Mrs Becky Totterdell of SU Publishing for her helpful work in editing the manuscript.

Above all, I want to thank my wife Hazel and our sons Craig and Stuart for their encouragement and support while I wrote it, despite the hours it took out of our time together as a family.

Start Here . . .

When we read the Bible we usually do so with all kinds of ideas and questions buzzing around in our minds. This is especially so if the passage we are reading is one that we know to be difficult or controversial, like Genesis 1–11 which we will study in some detail. These ideas and questions can be a hindrance to understanding what we read. They can act like a fog, preventing us seeing things clearly and confusing us so that we go down the wrong paths. That is why this book does not start by going straight to Genesis 1:1 and asking, 'What does it mean?' Instead we begin with some fog dispersal. It will take some time but the result will be worth it when we turn our attention to Genesis 1–11.

This book is about Genesis and how far scientific discoveries can help us to understand it. Many people have only the vaguest ideas about what science is and about what it can and cannot tell us. This is true even of some scientists! Few have a clear idea of the nature of scientific theories and laws and how they are related. Yet the arguments that surround Genesis are full of references to such things as the *theory* of evolution and the second *law* of thermodynamics. So we must spend some time dispersing the fog that surrounds science in many people's minds. I will do this as clearly and simply as possible without over-simplifying. None of this will require you to have much knowledge of science, just a willingness to think about what you read!

Some people are confused about the nature of the Bible, how it should be interpreted and what we can and cannot expect it to tell us. Here, too, some fog dispersal is needed. Even if you have been a reader of the Bible for some time you should find this a useful refresher course on understanding the Bible. It will equip you to look more carefully at those chapters about whose interpretation there is some disagreement.

It would be foolish and arrogant to claim that this book will solve all the problems of Genesis 1–11 for you. What I hope it will do is present clearly the different interpretations held by Bible-believing Christians, and their strengths and weaknesses. Inevitably, my own preferences will become clear. However, the aim is that by the end of the book you will be better able to come to your own conclusions on the basis of a clearer understanding of the alternatives.

So, if you are sitting comfortably, we will begin . . .

CHAPTER 1
Looking for Truth

It was a warm summer evening. Two people were walking along the beach listening to the gentle lapping of the waves and looking at the star-studded sky. They both spotted a light flashing out at sea. One of them was a retired physicist, the kind of scientist who thought of nothing but his work. Science was his life. He rushed to his car where, being the sort of person he was, he kept all kinds of scientific equipment. He got out a stop watch and timed the flashes. He got out a photometer and measured the brightness of the flashes. He set up a spectrometer and recorded their spectrum. He noted the position of the light against the background stars. As he drove home along the coast road he stopped a couple of times and noted its position again, doing some triangulation calculations. When he got home his wife said, 'You look excited dear, did you see something interesting tonight?' 'Yes,' he said, 'I saw what I deduced was a heated tungsten filament, enclosed in a silica envelope, emitting a regular pattern of flashes of visible radiation at an intensity of 2,500 lumens from a distance of about 850 metres offshore.'

The other person on the beach that night was a teenager going home from Sea Scouts. When he got home his mother said, 'You look excited dear, did you see something interesting tonight?' 'Yes,' he said, 'I saw a boat signalling SOS and telephoned the coast-guard, and they sent out the lifeboat.'

Which of these two people gave the more accurate description of what they both saw? Neither. They each gave a perfectly accurate description but in quite different terms. The physicist described it in the only way it could be described within the bounds of the language, concepts and quantities recognized in physics. To have said more would have been to become 'unscientific', in the sense of going beyond what a physicist could say purely as a physicist. Physics can measure and talk about flashes of light; it knows nothing of Morse code and SOS. Such things belong to a different area of human experience.

The limitations of science

What this story illustrates is that physics, and indeed all science, has its limits. It works with carefully defined, and therefore strictly limited, methods and concepts. These restrict the kind of questions that scientists can ask and answer while using a scientific approach. Scientists are concerned with the physical world of matter and energy. They limit themselves to what can be counted, weighed and measured. As far as possible they try to express their findings in terms of mathematical equations. In other words, science is concerned with how the physical world works, its mechanism. Truly scientific questions can always be expressed as 'How?' questions. The physicist in our story was answering the question, 'How were the flashes of light being produced?'

There are, however, many other types of question that we want to ask. In some situations they are much more important than the 'How?' questions. For the people in the boat it was much more important that the Sea Scout asked, 'Why is somebody flashing a light?' and 'What do the flashes mean?' Fortunately for them he could read the message and understand its meaning because he knew Morse code, even though he may have known little physics.

By itself science can never answer questions of meaning, the 'Why?' questions. Scientific attempts to answer them always end up as 'how' answers. Suppose a medical doctor were asked, 'Why did Captain Oates die on the way back from the South Pole with Captain Scott?' He could only give a definite answer if he could find the body and carry out a post-mortem examination. Then he would no doubt say, in the correct medical terminology, that he died of extreme cold, frost-bite and the other effects of exposure to the Antarctic weather, which caused his body to stop functioning. That is really a mechanistic 'how'-type answer, how the Antarctic conditions affected his body with the result that he died. It says nothing about the meaning of this death in human and moral terms: an act of self-sacrifice in an attempt to free his friends of the hindrance of a sick man, in the hope that they could then travel faster and reach base camp before their resources ran out.

Many of the problems people have regarding science and the Bible result from the failure, or refusal, to understand the limitations of science. We live in a culture that has been affected deeply by 300 years of largely successful scientific endeavour. Among other things, it has affected the popular idea of truth. For most people scientific knowledge is *the truth*. There are a number of reasons for this: the success of science, the preciseness of most scientific explanations, the fact that (usually) scientists can agree about their answers whilst other people (eg politicians, economists, theologians) cannot. These and other reasons have given scientific truth considerable prestige. This has led to two widely held assumptions.

The first is that in areas of human experience that are not open to scientific study, especially morality and religion, truth is either purely relative ('if it makes you happy that's fine, but don't force your views on me') or non-existent. The public debate about AIDS gives evidence of this. It has centred on 'safe sex', how to avoid getting AIDS, but ignored discussing what forms of sexual activity are *morally* right or wrong – because there is no widely accepted basis for making such moral decisions. Science is looked to for a purely practical solution to the problem, such as a vaccine against AIDS.

Secondly, anyone or anything that seems to question, or disagree with, current scientific ideas is to be regarded with suspicion or discounted as wrong. Since the Bible seems at odds with modern scientific ideas in some places, especially the early chapters of Genesis, it is ignored or rejected as being out of date.

If we can see the limitations of science we can see that these assumptions are wrong and therefore harmful. The methods and terms of reference of science prevent it from investigating questions of value and meaning, the questions with which morality and religion claim to deal. But this does not mean that questions about value and meaning are not worth asking. Nor does it follow that there are no moral or religious truths. What it does show is that in these areas truth has to be reached by other means.

Limited in providing values

How valuable is a human being? Apparently most people think humans have some value because they think that murder is wrong. The law says that it is wrong to kill a person but not wrong to kill and eat a chicken. How can a scientist put a value on a human being?

A chemist might analyze a human body in terms of its chemical constituents. However, to 'value' it one would have to bring in the external, non-scientific, criterion of the market value of the chemicals. This would put a premium on those with gold fillings in their teeth!

A zoologist might think in terms of humans being one of the most recent products of the process of the evolution of life on earth. But why should the most recent product be the most highly valued? Why not put most value on, say, the species that has been around longest? At least it has shown staying power! We might be tempted to value humans in terms of the size of their brains in relation to body size. But why choose that criterion instead of, say, running speed? The best the zoologist can do is to rank humans alongside other life forms in terms of certain characteristics; we have to go outside of science in order to put any value or moral significance on these characteristics.

A social scientist might try to argue that murder is 'wrong' because it destabilizes and disrupts society. But why should it be 'good' to have a stable society? A moral position is being assumed here without it being argued for on any scientific grounds. We might argue that it is 'convenient' for most people if society is stable but a murderer can equally well argue that it was 'convenient' (perhaps in financial terms) to kill the victim. Whose convenience is to be given preference?

Moral philosophers have, of course, discussed questions like this at great length. The great majority would agree that science (the study of 'what is', the way things are) cannot serve as a basis for deciding moral values ('what should be', the way things ought to be done). Questions of value have to be decided on other grounds. Some atheistic philosophers even admit that if there is no God there are no rational, universal grounds for morality or meaning. The influential philosopher Jean-Paul Sartre wrote,

'The [atheistic] existentialist finds it extremely

embarrassing that God does not exist, for there disappears with him all possibility of finding values in an intelligible heaven' (*Existentialism and Humanism*, p 33).

Sartre's reference to the 'intelligibility' or meaningfulness of life brings us to the other major limitation of science. It cannot answer questions such as, 'What is life all about? Is there any meaning to it all?'

Limited in giving meaning

Our belief that there is meaning to life is closely linked to our reasoning ability, and so with rationality. But why should we trust our minds or indeed those of the scientists whose conclusions we so readily accept as 'reliable knowledge'? Is there any scientific basis for this trust? The simple answer is, no.

The most that science can do is tell us how our brains work: the physics and chemistry of what goes on in our brain cells. Science cannot tell us the meaning of these physical and chemical happenings in terms of reason and logic. We are back to our story. The physicist could say how the flashes of light were produced but nothing about the message they carried.

Some people have argued that if our thought processes can be explained in terms of physics and chemistry, and so in terms of apparently fixed laws of nature, then our thoughts are completely determined by these laws. There is no such thing as free will. When Professor Taylor, a mathematician at London University, argued this way in

New Scientist magazine in 1971, he received this riposte in the letters column from one of the magazine's readers:

> 'Prof. Taylor's resolved our confusion
> and proved that free will's a delusion.
> But though he has said it
> He can't expect credit,
> Since he's programmed to draw this conclusion.'

If the scientific explanation of our thought processes is the only one, then Professor Taylor is right and our thoughts are completely determined. The reader is also right: we have no grounds for believing or accepting what other people say. They have to believe what they do and if it differs from what I believe, there is no way of resolving the difference – it is rooted in the physics and chemistry of our brains, not in logic. The eminent physicist Professor J Haldane recognized this a long time ago, when he wrote,

> 'If my mental processes are determined wholly by the atoms in my brain I have no reason to suppose that my beliefs are true. They may be sound chemically, but that does not make them sound logically. And hence I have no reason for supposing my brain to be composed of atoms. In order to escape from this necessity of sawing away the branch on which I am sitting, so to speak, I am compelled to believe that mind is not wholly conditioned by matter' (*Possible Worlds*, p 209).

He went on to say that it is necessary to believe in an 'infinite mind' existing 'behind nature' in order to explain the existence of human rationality.

A child of Christianity

Here, then, we can see that logic and reason, which are fundamental to the whole scientific enterprise, cannot be explained or proved reliable by science itself. Their value has to be assumed by scientists. But on what grounds? Historically the answer to that question is quite clear. The founders of modern science believed in reason and in its ability to understand nature on thoroughly Christian grounds. In fact one philosopher, Professor J MacMurray, claimed that 'Science is the legitimate child of a great religious movement, and its genealogy goes back to Jesus' (*Reason and Emotion*, p 172). This may seem a strange thing to say today, when many people have the impression that science and Christianity are to some extent rivals. However, historians and philosophers of science over the last fifty years have made it increasingly clear that modern science owes a great debt to Christianity.

Of all the great civilizations that the world has known, why was it that modern science was born in Christian Europe at the end of the Middle Ages? The knowledge about the world and the technical expertise possessed in other cultures were not in themselves enough to get science going, as we know it. The Greeks, the Hindus of the Ganges valley, the Arabs and others had considerable knowledge and technical expertise but never developed science as an ongoing movement. What was missing was the right framework of thought which would give people the confidence and motivation to allow scientific study to flourish.

This was eventually provided by Christianity. This is why a leading historian of science says:

> 'The scientific quest found fertile soil only when faith in a personal, rational Creator had truly permeated a whole culture, beginning with the centuries of the High Middle Ages. It was that faith which provided, in sufficient measure, confidence in the rationality of the universe, trust in progress, and appreciation of the qualitative method, all indispensable ingredients of the scientific quest' (S Jaki, *Science and Creation*, p viii).

The Bible teaches that the world was created by God out of nothing as an act of his free will (Hebrews 11:3). It depends on him for its continued existence moment by moment (Hebrews 1:3). Since God acted as a free agent and we cannot presume to be able to predict what he would have done, the only way we can find out about and understand his creation is by studying it through observation and experiment.

The God of the Bible is a personal, rational and faithful Creator. Therefore his creation can be expected to be orderly and rational. Passages such as Genesis 1 and 8:22 support this conclusion. It was on this basis that the early scientists developed the concept of natural laws and began to look for them.

According to Genesis 1:26–27 human beings are made in the image and likeness of God. This gave the early scientists confidence to believe that their minds were finite reflections of God's mind and that they would therefore be able to understand his creation and his natural laws. They did have grounds for relying on human reason and logic.

The command of Genesis 1:28 to rule over the earth, and of Genesis 2:15 to take care of the garden of Eden, gave a religious motivation for scientific study of nature. It was seen as a way of carrying out these commands. Indeed it was seen by some as a way of co-operating with God to repair some of the damage done to nature by the disobedience of Adam and Eve.

Of course, only a minority of scientists today understand or accept this Christian framework for what they are doing. That is one reason why there is considerable debate amongst philosophers of science about the nature and basis of scientific truth. The fact is that originally the scientific enterprise found its purpose and meaning outside of itself, in Christian theology. Today, with that purpose and meaning largely neglected, it is not possible to find any other widely acceptable basis for science.

Conclusions

Three things become clear from this look at the nature of scientific truth, its limitations and its basis.

Science cannot explain everything

Firstly, the person who is sceptical about Christianity and tempted to believe that science provides the explanation for everything should be more cautious. We have seen that that belief is at best muddle-headed and at worst self-defeating.

It is a muddle-headed belief because it fails to recognize the self-imposed limitations of science and therefore the wide range of questions which science cannot answer. These questions are worth serious exploration by non-scientific means before they are written off as pointless. After all, down the centuries many people have found the answers to them to be of more importance than scientific knowledge!

It is a self-defeating belief if, recognizing the limits of science, it still insists that scientific truth is *the* truth. We have seen that this insistence undermines all belief in rationality and so undermines science itself.

Science explores God's truth

Secondly, Christians who are suspicious about, even afraid of, science should be encouraged to take a more positive attitude to it. Although the great majority of scientists today are not Christians, modern science is 'the legitimate child of Christianity' and there is nothing inherently anti-Christian about it. In fact, to some extent we can point to the success of science as evidence of the truth of the Christian beliefs upon which it was founded. When Christianity is attacked in the name of science, it is usually being attacked on grounds that are not purely scientific. Generally an anti-Christian philosophy lies behind the scientific jargon, with scientific facts being brought in to make the argument sound scientific. Christians have nothing to fear from facing up to the established findings of science because they are facts about God's creation. As such they will eventually fit into the overall picture of his truth.

Of course, it is not always easy to distinguish between the 'established findings' of science and those that are more provisional. Upheavals in thought over the last one hundred years – relativity and quantum mechanics in physics and plate tectonics in geology, for instance – have taught scientists the danger of presumption and the need for open-minded humility. Some have not learnt the lessons very well! We will return in the next chapter to this question of how much reliance we can put on particular scientific findings and theories.

God the creator is still necessary

Thirdly, we need to look at one particular area in which the limitations of the scientific approach are obvious. Modern science contains theories about the origin of the universe, the origin of the solar system and, of course, the origin of life on earth. All these are expressed in purely materialistic terms without any reference to God, so does this mean that scientists have shown that a creator God is unnecessary? Some scientists (eg P Atkins in *The Creation* and R Dawkins in *The Blind Watch-Maker*) claim that they have. However, they are forgetting the limitations of science and claiming too much. The most that a scientist can claim for a theory about the origin of the universe, for example, is that it explains *how* God, if he exists, brought the universe into being; what mechanism he used. It certainly does not explain away the need for the God of the Bible. Christians believe in a God who thought up and brought into being matter, energy and time and the fundamental laws and forces of nature which govern their behaviour. Moreover, he continues to keep them in being. He was free to bring the universe into being by whatever process he chose and the scientist is free to study the universe to see if that process can be discovered and understood.

Similarly, it is possible that God chose to bring all or some life forms into being through what biologists call the process of evolution. It would not make him any less the creator if he did so. An engineer, for example, could design and build a robot that could then design and build an even more complex robot. Could not the engineer legitimately claim to be the inventor of the more complex robot? Archbishop Geoffrey Temple was questioned about the implications of the theory of evolution when it was still quite novel. He reportedly replied, 'We used to believe in a God who made things. Now we must believe in a God who made things make themselves.' He could not see that this was any challenge to belief in a creator. Which God is in fact the more awesome – one who just makes things or one who can make things make themselves?

Facing up to apparent clashes

At this point some Christians might be feeling a bit unhappy. Surely the Bible tells us *how* God created the heavens and the earth and all living things? And doesn't it tell a rather different story from that told by modern science? Answers to these questions are going to take up the major part of this book. So here we will simply mention that when there is an apparent clash between science and the Bible at least three possible conclusions could be drawn:

1 The Bible might be right and the scientists wrong. Scientific theories do come and go, and occasionally there are radical changes in scientific views. Christians should not be slavish followers of scientific fashion. It is important that Christians in science should be prepared to ask radical questions about accepted scientific orthodoxy and should oppose scientific arrogance and prejudice, provided they do this in a truly scientific way.

2 The scientists might be right and the Bible wrong. Some Christians have taken this view with regard to the early chapters of Genesis and so have had to give up the traditional Christian doctrine of the Bible as God's word. Those who believe that the Bible is indeed the inspired word of the creator whose glory is revealed in nature, will never regard this as a necessary option. Ultimately it must be possible to harmonize scientific truth and biblical teaching.

3 The scientists might be right and our interpretation of the Bible might be wrong. Just as scientists need humility, so do Christians! However traditional and cherished our particular understanding of a Bible passage may be, it is still only our interpretation of it and it might be mistaken. If the scientists show us that it is mistaken, then we should be grateful to them for helping us to take a step nearer to a true understanding of God's word.

CHAPTER 2
Ways of Seeing

There was once a man who thought he was dead and he went about telling people so. Understandably, his relatives engaged a psychiatrist to try to convince him that he was deluded. The psychiatrist eventually hit on what seemed a sure way of dispelling the man's delusion. He decided to begin by convincing his patient that dead men do not bleed. He therefore sent him off to the local library with a list of medical books to consult, took him to talk with eminent doctors and took him to visit some hospitals to see post-mortems performed. Eventually the man admitted that he was utterly convinced that dead men do not bleed. At this the psychiatrist produced a knife and slashed his patient's arm, which bled profusely. The man stared at his bleeding wound, turned very pale and eventually stammered, 'Dead men *do* bleed!'

If someone believes something very strongly, he will do all he can to force the evidence to the contrary to fit in with his belief, rather than change his mind. Scientists are not supposed to be like that. The traditional, widely held view of how the scientist arrives at his conclusions is something like the following.

The scientist begins by collecting observational data in a purely objective way, free from all prejudices about the subject being studied, with no preferences concerning what theory might be correct and not hampered by any religious or philosophical ideas. In time, hopefully, some order or pattern will become apparent in the data. This the scientist will try to summarize (preferably in a mathematical form) as a law. Then, by a process known as induction, the scientist will try to arrive at some wider generalizations and principles to connect together several laws. This produces a theory. In some cases more than one theory might emerge. The scientist will then try to deduce from the different theories some predictions which can be tested by observation. Hopefully, eventually the predictions of only one theory will stand up to testing.

Scientific teaching about the world

This account of the scientific method has some truth in it. Apart from anything else it does draw attention to some of the characteristics of science. So far we have used the term 'science' without really defining it. In fact it is not easy to define. That does not mean that it is a meaningless or useless term. Try defining what you mean by 'love'. It is not easy, but that does not stop us saying, 'I love you' or being able to tell the difference between a loving and an unloving action. While there is no simple, agreed definition of science, there are certain characteristics which are generally agreed to mark certain types of activity or pieces of work as 'scientific'.

Firstly, science is concerned with the natural world of material things and events. Moreover, it looks for explanations of these things and events in terms of matter and energy alone. This separates science from philosophy and theology; science is concerned with the mechanism of the world but philosophy and religion are interested in such things as meanings, purposes and values.

Secondly, science is based on what actually happens in the natural world – which is studied by observation and experiment. It may be fun to dream up a bright idea and then theorize about its possible implications but that is simply science-fiction unless the idea can be shown to be rooted in events in the material world.

Thirdly, the links which scientists make between pieces of data or between laws, have to be rational ones. Using mathematics to describe what they think is happening is one way of ensuring this.

Scientists aim to be objective in their work. In other words they try not to let their own personal preferences or beliefs influence them. For this reason only those observations and experiments which can be repeated by other people (under suitable conditions and with relevant training) are acceptable as scientific data.

A lot more could be said about the nature of science but for our purposes it is enough to say that it is the attempt to carry out by observation and experiment an objective study of the material world aiming at rational, materialistic explanations of what goes on in that world.

Facts and theories

Our description of how scientists work is a description of the ideal. In practice no one does, or could, work that way.

Scientists are always selective in the data or 'facts' which they collect. This may be because they can only spend limited time or money in searching for the data. Besides this, they will usually have a particular reason for making the observations or doing the experiment, often the desire to prove or disprove a theory. This means that before they start looking they already have an idea of the sort of data they want to find. The way a person has been trained and her past experience will also affect the way she sees and collects data. This can be a good thing. A doctor can see significant things in an X-ray picture which a non-medical person would not. Of course, this training can mean that a person comes to the data with certain fixed expectations which blind her or him to some aspects of it. Similarly, if a scientist is committed to a particular theory he or she can, quite unwittingly, overlook data or see it in a biased way, a bit like the 'dead' man in our story.

All in all, scientists are becoming much more aware that the line between facts and theories is a fuzzy one. Theories are attempts to make sense of facts but what we see as facts, and how we assess them, is affected by the theories we already hold (or reject). As philosophers of science sometimes put it, all facts are to some extent 'theory-laden'.

Theories and reality

There is much debate today among philosophers of science about whether scientific theories tell us anything about the real world and, if they do, in what way. To a large extent this debate arises because of the loss of the Christian basis for science. Certainly the Christian believes that the scientist is studying a *real* world with a mind which is patterned on that of the world's creator and which can therefore understand the world as it really is. So the Christian will accept that what scientists tell us about the world does indeed correspond to reality.

However, the relationship between a theory and reality is not simple and straightforward. On the one hand the fact that some theories last for centuries, successfully accounting for all the available data, might lead us to regard theories as simple descriptions of reality. On the other hand, since some theories come and go very quickly, we might be tempted to think of theories as not much more than figments of the imagination, soon dispelled by a dose of reality. The truth is somewhere in between these extremes.

There are two ways of thinking about scientific theories that are quite popular at the moment. One compares them to maps. In my map of London every symbol corresponds to some real feature of London. The red lines correspond to roads and the thickness of the lines to the width of the roads. The blue areas correspond to ponds, lakes and rivers. When I show someone the map I do not claim that it *is* London, but I do claim that it corresponds to a real city and will enable them to find their way around it. Similarly, it is argued, scientific theories are not to be confused with reality itself but they do correspond to it, and help us to find our way around in it.

Another way of looking at theories is to regard them as mental 'models'. Most people, including most scientists, find it easier to think in pictures than in words or mathematical equations. For this reason many 'models' used by scientists are mental pictures. For example, one can think of a gas in terms of the 'billiard ball model'. This sees a gas as a lot of miniscule billiard balls in an enclosed box, always moving about, bouncing off each other and the walls of the box. In fact, by applying Newton's laws of motion to this model it is possible to obtain a fairly good mathematical description of how gases actually behave. But no one believes that gases really *are* made up of miniscule billiard balls. There is a lot of evidence to prove otherwise! The model is not a simple description of reality but key features of the model do correspond to features of the real world. In this way the model helps us to understand and control the world. We only have refrigerators in our homes because the scientific model of how gases behave showed how they could be used as coolants.

This discussion of the nature of scientific theories has two important things to say to us as we consider how scientific knowledge and the Bible relate to one another. It tells us that we cannot simply brush aside scientific theories by saying, 'Oh, that's only a theory!' Good theories do relate to the realities of the material world. On the other hand it warns us not to tie our understanding of the Bible too closely to any one theory, because theories are only representations of reality and will come and go as science advances.

This faces interpreters of the Bible with a dilemma. 'How far should I go in taking theory x into account, since theories come and go?' There is no simple answer to this but there are some useful guidelines.

Firstly, every theory has been produced to account for a set of data. Even if we do not take the theory into account we will probably have to take note of the data. When a theory is discarded, the data on which it is based do not disappear but have to be explained in some other way. For example, the theory of evolution arose largely to account for the fossil data. If we reject the theory of evolution, whether for biblical or scientific reasons, we have to provide an alternative theory that explains the fossil evidence.

Secondly, whether we like it or not we have to say something about those theories which are well-known and widely held. People will not take us seriously in other areas unless we do. They will see us as irrelevant, avoiding the issues which interest them.

Thirdly, at any one time there are those theories which responsible scientists regard as well-established and which provide a reliable basis for further scientific advance. We have got to take these seriously. We must see what their implications are, if any, for our interpretation of the Bible and for Christian thought. An example of this is the quantum theory and its implication that 'chance' or 'random' events play an important part in the fundamental processes of the universe. We will look at this later.

Testing theories

A theory links together laws, which in turn are derived from observational or experimental data. So theories stand at some distance from the data. What is a good theory and how does a theory come to be regarded as well-established?

There are a number of characteristics which scientists look for in a good theory. They are:

- *Consistency*. There should be no logical contradictions between the different parts or concepts which make up the theory.
- *Coherence*. It should be possible to make a variety of connections between the different concepts within the theory and with other theories.
- *Simplicity*. The number of assumptions involved should be small. Almost any theory can be made to work if enough arbitrary assumptions are allowed!
- *Comprehensiveness*. It should help us to see a unity underlying apparently diverse phenomena. If a theory can absorb the theory it replaces that is a strong point in its favour. For example, the theory of relativity includes Newton's theory of gravity as a special case.
- *Fruitfulness*. Scientists are most interested in theories which suggest new ideas, concepts, laws

and experiments rather than those which simply summarize existing ones.

• *Elegance*. This is hard to define. It often refers to the way in which the theory can be expressed mathematically.

However well a theory scores in terms of these six characteristics, scientists will want to test it experimentally. This is done by using the theory to make predictions which can be tested in some way. These, of course, should be predictions that rival theories do not make. For instance, Einstein's theory of relativity predicted that light should be bent by massive bodies such as the sun. Newton's theory of gravity did not predict this. It was the observation of such bending of light by the sun which convinced many physicists that Einstein's theory had to be taken seriously.

A theory may stand up to many such tests but it can never be said to have been absolutely proved. It is always possible that someone will think of yet one more test which will cause it to fail – as was the case with Newton's theory of gravity after more than 200 years. A theory can be disproved by its failure in just one test but it can never be proved conclusively. All the same, it seems reasonable to have more confidence in a theory the more tests it passes.

At this point it must be said that a theory is not always immediately abandoned simply because it fails a single experimental test. It may be that the failure can be overcome by a fairly minor modification of the theory. Even if this is not the case, a theory that has stood for quite a while and proved to be useful will not be readily abandoned until there is something better to put in its place. Scientists would rather work with a theory that they know is somewhat defective than have no theory at all. It is this reason, and not just stubbornness or obscurantism, that makes biologists cautious about throwing over the theory of evolution although there are discrepancies and loose ends in it. At the moment they are not convinced that there is anything better with which to replace it.

If it is true that theories are maps or models of reality, then we can assume that as better theories replace earlier ones, scientists are achieving better and better representations of, or approximations to, the reality of the material world.

It is sometimes claimed that theories of origins (of the universe, of life) are in a different class from other theories because they relate to unique, unrepeatable and, for us, unobservable events. However, it is not clear that this makes them all that different. Few theories, if any, relate to readily repeated and observed events in a simple, direct way. Theories of origins can be evaluated by the six criteria listed earlier in the same way as other theories. They, too, can be tested by their predictions.

The 'big bang' theory of the origin of the universe proposed that the universe began with a massive explosion of energy. As things cooled down various atoms were formed. These then formed gas clouds, out of which galaxies and stars came into being. Among other things, this explained the apparent expansion of the universe which is observed today. In the 1960s this was opposed by the 'steady state' theory. This said that as the universe expands new matter appears in space to keep the density of matter in the universe more or less constant. The big bang theory triumphed because it predicts that radio astronomers should be able to observe background radiation left over from the initial 'big bang'. They have done this. The steady state theory does not predict the existence of this radiation.

Scientific laws

So far we have said little about scientific laws or 'the laws of nature,' as they are often called. There is one misconception about them which needs to be cleared up.

Unfortunately the word 'law' is used in science in a rather different way from its everyday use. In common speech a law is a *prescription*, a statement about what you are supposed to do or not do. The speed limit laws are an example. In science a law is a *description*. It is a statement about a pattern that has been observed in the way things happen in the material world. It is like the statement of someone doing a road survey who says that ten per cent of the motorists were travelling faster than the speed limit. A scientific law does not say that this is the way things *have to happen* but simply that this is the way things *have been seen to happen* under certain circumstances in the past. This is why scientific laws, like theories, are always open to revision in the light of new observations and fresh understanding of the world. It is also why the laws of nature cannot be said to rule out miracles; but that is another story.

Christian teaching about the world

So far we have looked at understanding the world in purely scientific terms. Some may wonder whether there is any other way of understanding it. That brings us back to chapter 1 and the different questions which science and religion ask about the world. Science asks, 'How has the universe come about?' and may answer in terms of the big bang theory. Religion asks, 'Why is the universe here at all?' Christianity answers in terms of a creator God and his purposes. We will look more closely at this answer later in this book.

The scientific understanding of the world is expressed in theories which are ultimately derived from data or 'facts' about the world. These theories can be evaluated and tested, as we have seen. What 'data' or 'facts' provide the Christian 'theory' – Christian teaching? And how can that teaching be evaluated and tested?

The primary data for Christian teaching is the Bible, along with our experience of life in the world interpreted in the light of the Bible's teaching. This is not the place to discuss why Christians believe the Bible to be the inspired word of God and therefore reliable as the basis for their understanding of the world. For that you will need to go to other books. What we will discuss here is how Christian teaching can be evaluated and tested.

Doctrines as models

Philosophers of religion have pointed out that just

as scientific theories can be looked at as models, so can Christian doctrines.

Much Christian talk about God consists of mental pictures or models – God as father, judge, rock and so on. God is not literally a father or judge as we know them in human terms. He is obviously not a rock! These models pick out certain characteristics (source of existence, love, justice, reliability) and claim that they are true of the reality we call God. Talking of what Jesus has done for us as redemption or justification is also to use models, this time drawn from experience of the freeing of captives and acquittal in court.

Recognizing that Christian doctrines are like models of reality helps us to avoid equating them with the reality which they try to describe. Just as scientific theories are always open to revision or replacement in the light of new data, so Christian doctrines must be open to revision in the light of fresh understanding of the Bible.

The characteristics that are looked for in good theories also apply, with a little modification, to Christian doctrines: consistency, coherence, simplicity, comprehensiveness, fruitfulness, elegance.

At this point it might be objected that a doctrine like that of the trinity violates the characteristic of consistency, since surely there is a logical contradiction involved in talking about one God existing as three persons. Part of the answer to this is to define carefully what theologians mean by 'person', but we will not stop to do that here. Besides this we could say that it is not illogical when you recognize that the reality about which we are trying to speak is of a different, far more complex, order of being than we are. God is not limited to space, time and matter as we are. So we should not be surprised that talking about him stretches the capacity of our language and models. In fact, to make a reasonably adequate attempt to describe him as he has revealed himself to us in the Bible we have to use both the model of oneness and the model of three persons.

The use of such apparently incompatible models is known in science as well. The classic case is in the description of the behaviour of the electron. In some situations it is best described by the model of a particle, a miniscule billiard ball. In others it behaves like a wave, like a ripple in the water. The theory of the electron has to incorporate both models to do justice to all that is known about it. There is no logical contradiction involved because there are no situations when *both* models can be applied at the same time and give contradictory predictions. The doctrine of the trinity has been constructed carefully by Christian theologians so that it does not lead to self-contradictory 'predictions' or statements about God and his activity in the world.

Ultimately, scientific theories are tested by their 'fit' with the world. How well they fit is discovered by testing the predictions they make about the world. Christian doctrine is tested in much the same way. Does it make sense in my life as I live in obedience to it? Does it make more sense of the world than other religions or philosophies which clamour for attention? This does not make Christianity purely individualistic and subjective because I can, and should, take into account whether or not it makes sense of other people's experience too. This is like the need for the tests of scientific theories to be open to repetition by other people.

Another aspect of the objectivity of Christianity is its historical basis. A series of historical events lies at the heart of Christianity. Some of these are shared with Judaism because both religions share the Old Testament. However, the distinctively Christian event is the birth, life, death and resurrection of Jesus. Christians claim that this has to be taken into account in any attempt to explain the meaning and purpose of life in this world.

The rôle of faith

Faith plays a big part in both Christianity and science. Christianity is about having faith in Christ. This is often thought to highlight an irrational element in Christianity. Science, on the other hand, is supposed not to involve faith but to rest purely on what can be proved rationally.

There are two misconceptions here.

The first is that faith has no place in science. In fact it is fundamental to it. Scientists believe without absolute proof (that is, they have faith) that the world is ordered in a rational way and that this order is stable. Moreover, they believe without absolute proof (that is, they have faith) that the human mind is rational and can discover and understand that order correctly. It is not possible to do science without taking these basic steps of faith. We have seen that originally these beliefs were derived from Christian teaching. Without that basis they just hang in the air. It might be argued that they have been proved by the fact that they work. But do they work? Might not all scientists be suffering from a mass delusion like the 'dead man' at the start of this chapter? Some philosophers of science, having no time for the Christian basis of science, suggest as much.

Life as a Christian begins by putting one's faith in Christ as the saviour through whom we are brought back into a right relationship with our creator. The second misconception is to think that this act of faith is irrational. It is certainly a step beyond what can be proved with no shadow of doubt. However, most Christians would claim that it is a *reasonable* step. There is plenty of evidence in the Bible and in the experience of Christians down the ages that Jesus is who he claimed to be and that the commitment of one's life to him leads to the experience of God which is promised in the Bible. In other words, Christian faith is a reasoning and reasonable trust in Christ, based on a good deal of historical and experiential evidence which is available to those who wish to investigate it.

Complementary views of reality

We will end this chapter by considering how the scientific and Christian views of the world relate to each other. The simple way of putting this is to say that they are complementary views of reality. We need both of them in order to complete our understanding of reality. We need answers to both the 'How?' and the 'Why?' questions. These answers are neither contradictory nor mutually exclusive. They complement one another.

Physicists currently talk about fluctuations in a 'quantum vacuum' somehow snowballing and resulting in a 'big bang', leading to the universe as we know it. For the Christian this, if true, is simply a statement of how God chose to create the universe we know. Christian doctrine gives some reasons why he created it. We shall come to these in the second part of this book.

Scientists have discovered laws of nature. Some talk as if these somehow shut God out of the world and prevent him acting in it, if he exists at all. However, for Christians these are God's laws and he is free to override them if he wishes. But there is more to it than that. The Bible teaches that God did not just create the world and then stand back to let it get along on its own. He is constantly sustaining it. Perhaps the right way to think of the laws of nature is to see them as God's normal way of acting in his world, keeping it in being. Sometimes he may choose, for good reasons, to act differently – we call this a miracle.

We could go on showing how the scientific and Christian ways of looking at the world fit together. A picture that is sometimes used to help illustrate how they do this is that of the architect's plans for a building. The architect will draw up plans of the different levels – the ground-floor, the first-floor, and so on if there are others. There will be a front elevation, side elevations, a back elevation. Taken individually, these drawings may not seem to be related to each other but, to a person who knows what they are, they all fit together and make sense, giving an impression of the whole structure.

That illustration needs only one modification. The Christian view of reality is not just one architect's drawing on a par with others. It is more like the artist's impression of the finished building, which helps us to fit the other drawings together properly and make better sense of them. It is the overarching view. That view is found in the Bible and we will now turn to the question of how we make sure that we understand the Bible properly.

CHAPTER 3
Understanding the Bible

'The trouble with the Bible is that it can be used to prove anything!' The fact that people can make that complaint says more about the way the Bible has been used – or misused – than about the Bible itself. Just because the Bible has been regarded as the authoritative source for Christian belief Christians have all too often gone to great lengths to try to prove that it supported *their* point of view. As a result, some have ignored and violated all the normal rules of intepretation which they would apply when reading any other piece of literature.

Some Christians have been taught that they do not need to interpret the Bible. Professor Scholer of Northern Baptist Seminary in Chicago tells of an occasion when he preached in a church in Canada. As he greeted people at the door after the service one man said to him, 'I guess, Professor, it's all right for you to interpret the Bible, but I'll just do what it says!' That man did not realize that he *cannot* 'just do what the Bible says.' He does, or tries to do, what *he understands* it to say. Behind that understanding lies an interpretation of what he has read in the Bible.

Have you ever taken something that was not yours; been somewhere that you know as a Christian you should not have been; looked covetously at something that was not yours? 'Yes', is almost certainly your answer. So why have you still got two hands, two feet, two eyes? After all, Jesus said, 'If your hand/foot/eye causes you to sin, cut it off' (Mark 9:43–47). Why haven't you done what the Bible says?

'Hold on a moment,' you might say; 'you are being too literalistic. Jesus was using vivid picture language.' As it happens I think you are right, but in saying that you are interpreting the Bible. It is not a question of *whether or not* we interpret it, but whether or not we do it *consciously and properly*, following the basic rules of interpretation.

To speak of 'rules of interpretation' might make the Bible sound a difficult book, one that only scholars can safely read. That is not the case. The Bible's main message of salvation is clear and plain to all who read it wanting to find the truth. Besides which we take most of the rules of interpretation for granted anyway, because we apply them every time we read a newspaper, novel or notice on the church notice board. However, the Bible itself warns us that not everything in it is easy to understand. The apostle Peter says of Paul's letters,

> 'His letters contain some things that are hard to understand, which ignorant and unstable people distort, as they do the other Scriptures, to their own destruction' (2 Peter 3:16).

The Bible also refers to the need for effort and study if we are to learn how to handle the Bible properly. The apostle Paul says to Timothy,

> 'Do your best to present yourself to God as one approved, a workman who does not need to be ashamed and who correctly handles the word of truth' (2 Timothy 2:15).

So then, if we really do want to do what the Bible says, we will take seriously the task of learning how to interpret it.

An inspired Bible

Christians believe that the Bible is inspired by God. This is what the Bible claims for itself (eg 2 Samuel 23:2; Jeremiah 1:9; 2 Timothy 3:16). Some people think this means that God dictated the Bible to its authors, who were a bit like shorthand secretaries. But just a brief look at the contents of the Bible rules out this idea as too simplistic. There is clear evidence of very deep human involvement in the production of the Bible.

It seems that the writers of the historical books – books which tell the history of Israel – worked in the same way as other historians. They searched out sources, collated the information they gained, summarized some parts, quoted others in full, and so on. This is what seems to be implied by the frequent references to such sources (eg 1 Kings 11:41; 2 Chronicles 12:15). Luke tells us that he worked in a similar way when he wrote his Gospel (Luke 1:1–3). In the books of the prophets, the Gospels, and in the New Testament letters, the personalities of the writers are deeply woven into their writing. Each has his own writing style and his own favourite words and phrases (eg Matthew used the rabbinic phrase, 'the kingdom of heaven', which avoids using the word 'God'; Luke uses 'the kingdom of God'). The writers of the Bible used ordinary human languages. The Greek of the New Testament is the Greek that was used in the homes and market places of the eastern Mediterranean world of that time. The books of the Bible did not drop from heaven. They were the result of much human thought, effort and literary activity on the part of the writers.

To say that the Bible is inspired by God is to say that all this thought, effort and activity was guided by God. This is not to say that God in some way violated the normal thought processes or personalities of the writers. Nor does it mean that the Bible must contain errors put there by the human authors. If God knows each person's mind and personality inside-out, he could choose as writers those whom he knew would be able to understand what he wanted to convey and could pass it on without it becoming distorted.

In modern communications systems, as every telephone user knows, messages can be distorted by 'noise' in the system. If it is vital to avoid such distortion, experts can analyse the characteristics of the 'noise' and add to the message a signal which neutralizes the effects of the noise. The message then gets through undistorted. Surely God is capable of doing the same kind of thing when communicating his message to human beings!

The Bible, then, is a book that is both truly divine and truly human. It is its humanness that has to be taken into account in the task of interpretation; being written by real people it is rooted in particular historical and cultural situations and is expressed in languages and thought-forms that are not our own.

Interpreting the Bible

Where do we start? For most of us the starting point is an English translation of the Bible. This is not a trivial point. The Bible was written in Greek and Hebrew, with a few chapters in Aramaic. If we read it in English we are dependent to some extent on the translators' interpretation of the original. This is because any translation translates not just words but meaning. A word-for-word translation often makes little sense because it ignores the peculiarities in grammar and idiom of the two languages concerned. A word-for-word translation of the beginning of Leviticius 26:26 is: 'When I break for you a staff of bread.' That is good idiomatic Hebrew but does not make much sense as an English sentence! What the original means is: 'When I cut off your supply of bread.' A good translator cannot avoid doing some interpretation but will try to keep it to a minimum. A translation, such as the *New International Version* or the *Revised Standard Version*, differs from a paraphrase, such as *The Living Bible* or *The New Testament in Modern English* by J B Phillips. Paraphrases are freer translations which contain a high degree of the translator's own interpretation. They can be refreshing reading but should never be used as a basis for serious Bible study.

There are five rules to follow when trying to understand a Bible passage.

1 Compare translations

Compare the passage you are studying with the same passage in at least two other good modern translations. This way you will probably be able to spot the places where the translators' interpretation of the original has had a substantial effect on the translation. You can then take this into account in your study passage.

2 Use normal rules of language and literature

Interpret what you read in terms of the normal rules of language and literature. The fact that the Bible is God's word does not exempt it from these rules and enable you to make it mean whatever you want! On the contrary, God chose to express his message in the particular grammatical and literary forms that he did in order to fix its meaning in this way.

There are many different ways of using language. We are all used to making a distinction between poetry and prose and readily allow for 'poetic licence'. In poetry we expect to find words used in ways which, if taken literally, are nonsensical. What the writer is after is not the literal meaning but the images conveyed, the emotions aroused. To say, as the psalmist does a number of times, 'God is my rock, my fortress', is literal nonsense but the meaning is obvious to anyone with a grain of imagination.

It is not only in poetry that we use language in a non-literal sense. If I ask my wife how the day's teaching has gone and she says, 'I spent most of the afternoon banging my head against a brick wall', I do not start looking for the bruises! If her words are taken literally she has told me a lie. However, she has used language in a non-literal way to make a true statement about her experience in the classroom. This kind of 'figure of speech', as it is called, is in fact quite common in prose. We talk of a child being 'as bright as a button', of a friend as 'a tower of strength', someone else as 'a pillar of the church' and so on. These figures of speech are usually quite obvious to us in our own native language but are not always so easily spotted in a foreign language which may have its own, rather different set of images derived from its own cultural setting. This is a point to which we will return when studying Genesis 1–11.

Another aspect of this rule which we will need to consider when we come to look in detail at Genesis 1–11 is the importance of understanding and taking into account the type of literature which we are reading. The Bible is not a book but a collection of books. They are of many types: books of history, poetry, proverbs, prophecy, letters. Some books contain more than one type of literature. We can misunderstand a passage if we are not clear about the type of literature to which it belongs.

'What is a proverb?' I asked. 'A wise saying', 'A piece of good advice', were two of the answers I got. If that is so, what should we make of Proverbs 21:14? That verse reads:

'A gift given in secret soothes anger,
and a bribe concealed in the cloak pacifies great
wrath.'

Does this mean that we should give bribes? It does if proverbs are good advice – but they are not. Hebrew proverbs, at least, are *realistic observations* on life expressed in an easy-to-remember form. They do not necessary express a moral judgment. Proverbs 21:14 simply makes the observation that bribes sometimes succeed. This is what makes it so tempting to use them. However, Proverbs 17:23 does pass a moral judgment on the practice,

'A wicked man accepts a bribe in secret
to pervert the course of justice'.

This raises another important point. It is dangerous to take a small part of a passage or book and interpret it in isolation from the rest. The book of Proverbs' teaching on bribes cannot be decided on the basis of chapter 21:14 alone. We must consider all the proverbs about bribes which are contained in the book.

3 Harmonize rather than oppose

If we believe that the Bible is the inspired word of God we would not expect it to contradict itself, since we would not expect God, who is faithful and true, to say one thing at one time and then contradict himself at some other time. When we come across apparent contradictions (like Proverbs 17:23 and 21:14) we will expect that further thought and study will show how the two passages should be harmonized. However, we must not twist passages in order to force a harmony. Sometimes we just have to admit that we do not yet have an answer to the apparent contradiction. It may be that in time some fresh evidence or new insight will solve the contradiction.

4 Look for the original meaning

Establish what the passage would have meant to the original writer and his readers. To do this we have to learn all we can about the language, history and culture of the time. There are two aspects of this that will be of particular importance to our study of Genesis 1–11.

The form of literature

The first concerns the different forms of literature in the Old Testament. When discussing proverbs earlier I was careful to give the definition of a Hebrew proverb. In other languages and cultures proverbs might have a different character. The Hebrew proverbs in the Old Testament are similar in both form and content to Egyptian and Mesopotamian proverbs. We therefore have quite a large amount of proverbial material from the ancient near east, from which we can get a good idea of the nature and purpose of proverbs in those cultures. This gives a good basis for interpreting Old Testament proverbs correctly.

We need to treat the historical material in the Old Testament in the same sort of way. A good deal of similar material exists from ancient Egypt and Mesopotamia, from which we can discover the characteristics of history writing at that time.

Old Testament historical passages must be understood in the light of *these* characteristics, not in the light of how history is written in the twentieth century AD.

Similarly, when we look at Genesis 1–3 we will need to see whether other ancient near-eastern creation stories throw any light on the way in which these chapters should be understood.

Scientific and biblical literature

The second aspect concerns the different characteristics of scientific and biblical language. One mark of modern science is that it has developed its own kind of language. Scientists use words carefully – or should do. Terms are carefully defined and used as precisely as possible. In chapter 4 we will see that the way in which the words 'chance' and 'random' are defined in science is rather different from, and more precise than, their use in ordinary speech.

The Bible is not written in scientific language. On the whole, it is written in the popular language of the common people. There are exceptions to this in some of the terms used for the rituals of the temple in the Old Testament and in the more theological use of some words in the letters of Paul in particular (though these were written to ordinary people). The important point to note is that in the areas of most interest to science – where the Bible speaks about the natural world – the Bible uses popular language.

This language has three particular characteristics:

- *It is not very precise.* There have been

attempts to show that Genesis 1 teaches that species are permanently fixed and cannot evolve. This is because of the repeated statement that the plants and animals produced offspring 'according to their kind'. The Hebrew word 'kind' (*mīn*) is taken to mean the same as the scientific term 'species'. This just does not stand up to examination. Looking up a concordance to study the uses of the word *mīn* in the Old Testament makes it clear that its use is far too imprecise to equate it with any of the modern biological terms such as 'species', 'genera' or whatever. It is best translated by an imprecise English word such as 'kind'!

- *It is the language of appearance*, describing things as they appear to be to the ordinary observer. The Bible speaks of the sun 'rising' and 'setting', just as most people do today. (We do not, for instance, say, 'Look, because of the rotation of the earth the sun is disappearing below our line of sight.') The statement about animals reproducing 'according to their kind' probably expresses nothing more than the fact we all observe that dogs have puppies, not kittens. It should not be taken to rule out the possibility that major changes might occur over many generations.
- *It is full of cultural idioms*. Some reflect what might be called popular 'science', if you are prepared to stretch the meaning of 'science'. For example, there are frequent references in the Old Testament to people thinking, deciding, meditating on things 'in their heart'. There is no doubt that the Hebrew word here (*lēb*) does refer to the physical organ in the chest (eg 2 Kings 9:24). There is no known separate Hebrew word for 'mind'. It

may be that the Hebrews connected the heart with thought processes because sometimes there is a correlation between the rate of our heartbeat and what we are thinking. This is no different in principle from the way in which we link the heart with the emotions, because strong emotions affect our heartbeat. Scientifically, we are no more correct than the Hebrews. If emotions are to be connected with any bodily organ it ought to be with the endocrine glands. However, the Hebrews knew what they meant when they said, 'I pondered in my heart what to do', just as we know what we mean when we say, 'I love you with all my heart.' There is no problem unless someone insists that everything that the Bible says must be taken as scientifically accurate, totally ignoring the culturally bound, idiomatic use of language.

5 Look for the original intention

Finally, we come to our fifth rule of interpretation. This is that we must be guided in our interpretation by the author's original intention. What was he intending to talk about? To come back to our previous example, if it were clear that any of the Old Testament references to people thinking or planning in their hearts was *intended* to teach us about human physiology or psychology, then we would have a clash between the Bible and modern science. However, this was not the intention of those authors. Similarly, we will have to see whether there is any evidence to help us decide what the author of Genesis 1–3 intended to teach his readers. How far, if at all, was he concerned with explaining *how* God created the earth and living things? Was he perhaps only really concerned with telling us *why* God did it and what that means for the way we are to live our lives on earth? These are going to be crucial questions in the next chapter.

Truth and error

If the Bible is the inspired word of God in the way that we suggested at the beginning of this chapter, then we would expect it to be free from error. God knows everything so does not suffer, as we do, from ignorance. He is perfectly wise, so does not make mistakes. He is the truth, so will not lead us off course in our search for truth. For these kinds of reasons orthodox Christians have spoken of the Bible being 'infallible', 'inerrant', or 'trustworthy'.

At this point it is important to remember what we have discussed above about interpreting the Bible. Otherwise we will misunderstand the meaning of the 'inerrancy' of the Bible. If we misinterpret the Bible, it is not the Bible that is in error, we are. Listen to this sixteenth-century conversation between an astronomer (A) and a biblical scholar (BS):

A: I have proved that the Bible is wrong!

BS: Where? In what way?

A: In your commentary on Genesis 1:16, don't you stress that the Hebrew says, 'And God made *the* two great lights' and that this means that the sun and the moon are the two biggest heavenly bodies?

BS: Yes, that's true.

A: Well, using the newly invented telescope I have proved that the planet Saturn is much bigger than the moon. Therefore the Bible is wrong!

BS: It can't be! Your measurements and calculations must be wrong.

A: They're not! Two other astronomers have checked them. If you don't believe me come and see for yourself.

BS: No fear! The telescope is clearly an invention of the devil intended to lead people like you astray! I'm not going to look through it!

That conversation is not purely imaginary. This issue was being debated in the sixteenth century and John Calvin refers to it in his commentary on Genesis. He blames some scholars for making the Bible look silly by misinterpreting it and then insisting on the truth of their interpretation against all the evidence of the astronomers. In dealing with this issue Calvin appeals to two of the rules of interpretation we have discussed above.

The language of appearance

Firstly, he argues that the language used in Genesis 1, as everywhere else when the Bible speaks about natural phenomena, is the common language of appearance. The sun and the moon *appear* to be the largest and brightest of the heavenly bodies. All readers of Genesis down the ages have had no difficulty in understanding what is meant by 'the two great lights'. We know now that Jupiter is the biggest planet. If the language of Genesis 1:16 was meant to be scientifically precise, and so to refer to the sun and Jupiter (which seems impossible anyway, since how can Jupiter be said to 'rule the night' as the sun does the day?), all readers down the ages (and many today) would have been misled, since they were bound to think that the reference is to the sun and the moon.

Purpose

Secondly, Calvin insists that the purpose of Genesis 1, and indeed of the Bible, is not to teach astronomy but to lead us to see our need for salvation and to find it through faith in Christ. To think that astronomical information can be gleaned from Genesis 1 is to misunderstand the author's intention and so to misinterpret the passage.

Calvin's approach to this kind of issue is summed up by a comment he makes in his commentary on Psalm 136,

> 'The Holy Spirit had no intention to teach astronomy; and in proposing instruction meant to be common to the simplest and most uneducated person, he made use by Moses and other prophets of the popular language that none might shelter himself under the pretext of obscurity.'

Of course, Calvin was a man of his time and quite capable of making mistakes. For example, he assumed that for the moon to be a 'light' it must be a hot, burning body. After all, the lights that Calvin knew did all involve burning something (wood, oil, wax etc). We know now that the moon is only a reflector of sunlight. If the Holy Spirit had been interested in scientific instruction, surely Genesis 1:16 should have read, 'And God made a great light and a great reflector/mirror'!

It will be helpful at this point to sum up what we can learn from this example:

- Christians who believe that the Bible is free from error cannot claim that the same applies to their interpretations of the Bible.
- The claim that the Bible is free from error *must* include a proper understanding of the types of literature and language used in the Bible, and the original intention of the authors.
- If, as Christians, we are not scrupulously careful in our interpretation of the Bible and humble in the presentation of what we think it means, we will bring the Bible into disrepute by creating unreal errors in it. If we insist, as some medieval scholars did, that Genesis 1:16 must be taken literalistically (ignoring the kind of language used) as a source of astronomical information (ignoring the true purpose of the passage), then we have no defence when the astronomers turn round and say that they have proved that it contains two scientific errors about the size and nature of the moon.

Science and the Bible

We are now in a position to answer the question, 'How should we relate the findings of science to what we read in the Bible?'

First of all, what we have just said about interpreting the Bible warns us that we must be very careful in this area. We can only claim that a Bible passage provides information of a scientific kind when we are sure that this is warranted by the nature of the language in the passage, the type of literature to which it belongs, and the author's intention.

Secondly, if modern scientific findings seem to clash with the Bible, as we understand it, we must be prepared to re-examine our interpretation of the Bible. The scientists may be wrong and, if we have the expertise, we have the right to question and investigate the soundness of their claims. However, *we* may be wrong.

Just because the language of appearance is often the language of common sense, it is not always easy to recognize it except with hindsight. It seems obvious to us now that the biblical scholars who insisted that the Bible teaches that the earth is stationary and that the sun moves round it were reading the Bible in a wrongly literalistic way. But it was not so obvious to them partly because it seems common sense to see things that way: you know when you are on a moving cart, surely it would be obvious if we were on a moving earth! Three hundred years or more of modern science have taught us that common sense is not always a good guide to understanding the wonders of God's creation.

Science can in fact help us to avoid mishandling the Bible by helping us to recognize where we might be misinterpreting it. Some people are afraid that to talk like this is to subordinate the Bible to science. It is not. Perhaps an example from another area of study will help here.

A century or so ago there were a number of Greek words in the New Testament whose meaning was obscure. This was because they occur only rarely in the New Testament, in difficult contexts, and were not known in other Greek literature. Then, at the end of the last century a lot of Greek documents were discovered, preserved in the hot, dry sand of Egypt. Many of those obscure Greek words were found in them, in sentences where their meaning was clear. In some cases the meanings that had been proposed by New Testament scholars were confirmed, in others they were shown to be incorrect. No one would complain that the scholars were subordinating the Bible to language study by correcting their previous understanding of these words and so of the passages in which they occur. It was, rather, a case of subordinating their interpretation to the newly discovered truth. This is what we have to do with newly discovered scientific truth – once that truth has been well established.

This too is a principle which John Calvin recognized. In his *Institutes of the Christian Religion*, book 2, section 2.15 he says,

> 'If we hold the Spirit of God to be the only source of truth, we will neither reject nor despise the truth, wherever it may reveal itself, lest we offend the Spirit of God.'

The Bible is true but it does not contain all the truth about everything. God has given us minds and abilities to search for truth outside of the Bible. When we find it, it too is God's truth. We are then right to use it to help us understand the Bible more clearly – whether it be the results of language study, archaeology, history or even science.

The authority of the Bible

If the Bible is the inspired, inerrant word of God, then we ought to accept it as authoritative. We should listen to it, humbly accept what it says and then obey it. Does what has just been written about using truth from other sources to help us understand the Bible properly in any way lessen its authority? Not at all. The authority of the Bible is nothing other than the authority of God the Holy Spirit who inspired its writers. As we have seen, the same Holy Spirit is the source of all truth, which therefore bears his authority. To use that truth in interpreting the Bible is another way of submitting to the authority of the ultimate author of the Bible.

When Christians disagree

Finally, before we turn to our study of Genesis 1–11, we need to consider briefly the question of what we should do when we find that equally sincere and Bible-believing Christians differ from one another and from oneself in their understanding of what the Bible teaches. This, of course, is the case with Genesis 1–11.

I would suggest that, with God's help, we need to cultivate the following set of attitudes.

1 Humility. We need the humility to recognize that there may be a difference between what the Bible says and what we think it says. We may have misunderstood it and should be ready to re-examine, and perhaps, change, our interpretation.

2 Self-awareness. All kinds of factors predispose us to accept some interpretations while resisting others – our personality, background, experience, friends. Someone who works as a scientist may find it hard to question what the great majority of scientists simply accept as 'obviously' true. Most of us find it hard to question the interpretations of disputed passages of the Bible that are widely accepted among our Christian friends or in our church tradition. We need to ask God to search us and show us where we are being influenced by these kinds of factors and so not being truly open to his word in the Bible.

3 Integrity. Some people are unwilling ever to read or consider anything with which they think they might disagree, no doubt afraid that it might lead them to change their minds! This is an unhealthy and dishonest attitude. It is right for a baby to be protected for a while as it gains strength before exposing it to the world at large. Christians, however, should not remain perpetual babies (see Hebrews 5:11–14). We lack maturity and integrity if we hold strongly to a view without having given serious consideration to alternatives. In any case, we claim to be following a God who is the truth, so we have nothing to fear in examining all sides of an issue. Quite the reverse. Our desire, surely, is to discover the truth, his truth, not just to be proved right!

4 A sense of proportion. Does it really matter if Christians disagree? Yes, but it does not always matter to the same extent. As Christians we should be seeking to be one in Christ and so to agree with one another. However, the fact is that as long as we live in this world, limited by our finite minds and still not fully free from sin, we are going to disagree. But not all disagreements are of equal importance. Clearly the message of salvation by grace through faith in Christ is of central importance. Disagreements over that are very serious because they go to the heart of what it means to be a Christian. Disagreements over how God created the world, and whether or not the Bible tells us this, would seem to belong to a different category. In some circles, however, acceptance of particular views about this becomes almost a test of salvation: 'You are not really a Christian unless you have been saved by grace through faith in Christ *and* believe that . . .' I believe that this comes dangerously near to adding something to the gospel other than faith in Christ.

5 Love. Many disagreements can be lived with and then perhaps eventually settled, if those who disagree treat one another with love. We are called to love one another because Christ loved us enough to die for us, not because we agree with one another! That should enable us to pray, discuss, and live amicably, with those with whom we disagree while seeking to discover the truth together.

CHAPTER 4
Beginnings: A Literal Approach

Since the third century AD Christians have differed over whether or not Genesis 1 should be interpreted literally. Around AD 400 St Augustine of Hippo, one of the leading early theologians, argued in his commentaries on Genesis, his *Confessions* and in other writings, for a non-literal reading of the chapter. His reasons were theological, literary, and philosophical and obviously nothing to do with the theory of evolution!

It would require a very long book to describe and discuss all the various interpretations that have been offered for Genesis 1, not to mention the rest of chapters 1–11. We will therefore be simplifying and summarizing, with all the attendant risks of leaving out some ideas and arguments that others might consider important. The reading list at the end of this book gives a guide to other books that present various positions in more detail. Most of the different positions can be grouped into one of three types of approach: (1) literal; (2) concordist; (3) literary-cultural. In this chapter we will consider the literal approach but, before we do so, we need to look at three other matters.

An absolute beginning?

On the basis of Hebrew grammar alone it is possible to translate Genesis 1:1–2 in two different ways:

> '[1]In the beginning, when God created the universe, [2]the earth was formless and desolate.' (*The Good News Bible*).

> '[1]In the beginning God created the heavens and the earth. [2]Now the earth was formless and empty . . .' (*The New International Version*).

The difference between these is that the first allows the possibility that Genesis 1 begins not with nothingness but with the existence of unformed matter, to which God then gives form and order. In other words, it does not speak about the absolute beginning of the universe.

There are several reasons for preferring the second translation.

Firstly, verse 1 speaks of the creation of the earth or, more probably, everything (the phrase 'the heavens and the earth' is a Hebrew way of saying this, hence the translation 'universe'). It seems strange then to take verse 2 as meaning that the earth existed before this.

Secondly, elsewhere the Old Testament implies (eg Psalm 33:6–9; Proverbs 8:22–27; Isaiah 48:12–13) and the New Testament states (eg Colossians 1:15–17; Hebrews 11:3), that originally God alone existed and that the whole material world was brought into being by him. Therefore it did have an absolute beginning. It seems reasonable to interpret Genesis 1 in harmony with this.

Thirdly, this is how the majority of Jewish scholars (at least since the third century BC) and Christian scholars have understood the passage. It is particularly significant that this is how Jewish scholars understood it in pre-Christian times when Hebrew was still to some degree a living language. They were better placed than we are to judge how to understand this passage.

Creation from nothing?

Related to this issue of interpretation is a scientific one. Some scientists imply that since it now seems possible (though not yet certain) that the 'big bang' can be explained as arising from fluctuations in a 'quantum vacuum', science explains the ultimate origin of the universe. It does not and, in principle, cannot. A 'quantum vacuum' is not absolute nothingness. It is a kind of force field or energy field. Science has not explained the existence of such a 'vacuum', nor why it should have such characteristics as to make those fluctuations possible and why they should produce a universe. Any scientific explanation of these matters would have to be in terms of some prior situation or principles, which would then need an explanation, and so on. This is because, as we saw in chapter 2, science aims to give naturalistic explanations of what happens in the material world. It has to assume the existence of some kind of material world. According to the theory of relativity energy and matter are interchangeable, so a 'quantum vacuum' is a 'material world'. Logically and rationally, one is free either simply to accept the existence of that world without any kind of ultimate explanation for it or to believe (on other than purely scientific grounds) that God created it. Science can never deny the second possibility.

The Christian doctrine that God created the world 'out of nothing' does not mean that the 'nothing' is a kind of 'something' out of which God made the world. It is a shorthand way of saying that matter is not eternal (only God is) and that the world is entirely dependent on God for its existence.

God and chance

Some people find another problem in the fact that in modern scientific thought 'chance' or 'random' events play an important rôle in the fundamental process of the universe, from atomic physics to genetics. This seems to raise questions over the traditional Christian teaching about a purposeful creation and divine providence. Jacques Monod, winner of a Nobel prize for his work in molecular biology, claims that chance, not God, is the real creator,

> 'Chance alone is at the source of every innovation, of all creation in the biosphere. Pure chance, absolutely free but blind, is at the very root of the stupendous edifice of evolution' (*Chance and Necessity*, p 110).

Here Monod makes a classic logical blunder. He

treats 'chance' as if it were a positive force or cause, when it is quite the opposite. Scientists use the terms 'chance' and 'random' in a very specific way when referring to events. A chance event is one which cannot be predicted by scientists or can only be predicted in terms of statistical probability. What Monod is saying is really no more than that the genetic mutations that play an important part in evolution are events which scientists cannot predict. This does not mean that they have no cause (some of them are known to be caused by certain chemicals or types of radiation) or that God, if he exists, could not predict them.

A simple analogy may help here. A good spin bowler (all too rare in modern cricket!) will produce a variety of deliveries, the off-spinner, the top-spinner, the arm-ball, the straight ball. He will try to deliver them with little change in his delivery action and in a fairly random pattern. If he is successful the batsman will not be able to predict what kind of delivery it is until he is in mid-stroke. The batsman's inability to predict the delivery does not mean that the delivery is unplanned and lacking in purpose. What seems random from one point of view may be thoroughly purposeful from another.

We can see, then, that there is no contradiction between the importance of chance in the physical processes of the universe and belief in the providence of God at work in the world. The fact is that the Bible does not hesitate to regard what from a human point of view appear to be chance happenings, as being fully within the purpose of God. (For example, Micaiah the prophet predicted the death of Ahab, caused by an arrow fired at random: 1 Kings 22:17, 34; see also Proverbs 16:33).

As far as the question of design in nature is concerned, it is worth pointing out that random processes can be used purposefully. Modern designers use computerized 'random search' programmes to do certain design tasks, because they are the quickest and most efficient way of doing them.

A literal approach to Genesis 1:1–2:3

One of the ways of reading Genesis 1:1–2:3 (this is one of many examples of a biblical chapter division being put in an unfortunate place) is to take it literally, as a simple historical account of how God created the world. The attraction of this approach is that it seems so simple and obvious. It is the way most Christians have understood the chapter. Of course this is not conclusive. Christians traditionally took the references to the earth standing still to mean that it does not move and that the sun moves round it, until the findings of science showed that that interpretation had to be rethought. Besides which, as we have already noted, since the early Christian centuries some have questioned the literal reading of this passage. Since serious study of geology and the fossils began in the eighteenth century more and more Christians have questioned it.

Although the literal approach to Genesis 1:1–2:3

is simple in one way, it is far from simple in another. A vast body of literature has grown up to support it in the face of the findings of science over the last 200 years. There are three issues that have had most attention from those holding to the literal approach: the age of the earth, the fossils, and the theory of evolution.

Debate about the age of the earth and the fossils predates the theory of evolution. In fact before Darwin's *On The Origin of Species* was published in 1859 most Christian scholars, including those who held a high view of the Bible, accepted that the earth was millions of years old and sought to understand the opening chapters of the Bible in the light of that. The modern version of the view that the earth is only thousands of years old, not millions, seems to have originated in the 1920s with the Seventh-Day Adventist writer and teacher G M Price. It gained popularity in evangelical circles following the publication of *The Genesis Flood* by J Whitcomb and H Morris in 1961. Today this view is often referred to as the 'creation science' view. However, this is a bit misleading. Those who adopt both the other approaches we will discuss consider themselves 'creationists', and some would want to insist that their approach is also scientific. A more accurate description of this literal approach is to say that it is the 'young earth, flood geology' view.

The age of the earth

The reason that it is a 'young earth' view is that a simple, literal, reading of Genesis 1:1–2:3 cannot be divorced from a similar reading of the rest of Genesis, including the genealogies. Most people are aware of Archbishop Ussher's calculations based on these, which date the flood to 2349 BC and the creation of Adam to 4004 BC. Young earth advocates do not take these dates at face value. It would be difficult to do so since there are plenty of written historical records from Egypt and Mesopotamia which come from before 2000 BC and make it clear that the flood could not have happened in 2349 BC. Instead, it can be argued that the genealogies are selective and incomplete (as, for example, the genealogy of Jesus in Matthew 1 is seen to be, when compared with Old Testament genealogies). As a result those who hold the young earth view are usually happy to say that the earth was created about 10,000 years ago.

How then does this view deal with the scientific indications that the earth is about 4,000 million years old?

The earth simply 'appears' to be old

One way is to suggest that God created the world with an appearance of age. This idea goes back to a book entitled *Omphalos* written by P Gosse in 1857. Gosse argued that when God created Adam he presumably created him with a navel (*omphalos* is the Greek for 'navel') so that he looked just like someone born as a baby. Moreover, presumably the trees in Eden had growth rings, just as trees that have grown naturally since do and by which their age can be measured. In other words, a modern scientist transported back to Eden a few minutes after its creation would think that it had existed for decades or centuries. The same kind of argument can be applied to the geological strata, the fossils and all other indications of the age of the earth. There is no biblical evidence to help here, either for or against the theory.

If applied consistently this argument means that we must accept the findings of the scientists as accurate. They are measuring the age of the earth as God made it appear to be. To look for evidences of a different (younger) age would be to imply that God has been either inconsistent or incompetent in his creative work. The only way we can know the true age of the earth is from the Bible.

There are two difficulties with the view that the earth simply appears to be old. The first is that it means God's revelation in the Bible is to be taken at face value, though we are not to take his revelation in creation at face value. Secondly, and more seriously, it seems to make God guilty of deceiving even well-meaning investigators of his creation.

Some young earth advocates appeal to the appearance of age argument, yet also argue that there is evidence that the earth is only a few thousand years old. They seem not to realize that the two forms of argument are incompatible. As we pointed out earlier, if the earth was created to look old there should be no evidence that it is young.

Change of strength in magnetic field

A typical and popular example of the 'scientific' arguments for a young earth is that based on changes in the strength of the earth's magnetic field. In 1973 Dr T Barnes pointed out that the strength of the earth's magnetic field had decreased gradually over the previous 150 years. He plotted the values on a graph and then fitted what is called an 'exponential curve' (one whose value doubles at a fixed interval – every 1400 years in the case of Barnes' curve) to the data. Then he extrapolated this backwards in time, assuming that the magnetic field strength had decreased at a steady rate throughout the earth's history. He concluded that the strength would have been absurdly high 20,000 years ago. Hence the earth cannot be a great deal older than 10,000 years.

This conclusion, however, is not as obvious as it might at first appear to be, because there are a number of weaknesses in the argument.

Firstly, no scientist would normally extrapolate data by more than a factor of two or three. In other words, 150 years' worth of data would not normally be extrapolated back more than 500 years. This is because the slightest error in fitting the curve to the data gets magnified rapidly the further the data is extrapolated.

Secondly, Barnes' data are quite scattered and by no means fit his curve perfectly. In that situation an experienced scientist would not try to fit anything other than a straight line to the data. If this is done, the value of the magnetic field which Barnes regards as absurdly high is only reached after more than 100 million years.

Thirdly, any extrapolation depends on a steady change in the value being measured. It is doubtful that the rate of change of the magnetic field has been steady. For one thing, the variation in the earth's magnetic field is not the same from place to place. Over a 100 year period in Cape Town it decreased by thirty per cent. This would suggest that the earth is only a few hundred years old! Moreover, geologists think that there is very good evidence from magnetic rocks that the strength of the earth's magnetism has oscillated up and down, rather than decreased steadily. It last peaked about 2000 years ago. Before then it was increasing and since then it has decreased.

Fourthly, Barnes' view that the strength he calculates for the earth's magnetic field 20,000 years ago is absurdly high, depends on his theory of how the earth's magnetism is produced (the 'dissipating electric currents' theory). At present geophysicists favour a different theory (the 'self-sustaining dynamo' theory) of its origin. According to this the value calculated by Barnes is not absurdly high. However, it must be said that the question of how the earth's magnetism is produced is still far from settled.

These weaknesses in the argument have been pointed out quite often. It is unfortunate that some young earth advocates still refer to Barnes' argument as if it were quite conclusive, never mentioning the problems with it. This is not good 'science' and only brings creationism into disrepute, and the Bible with it.

On examination most of the arguments for a young earth seem to depend on questionable extrapolations of data or to rest on data whose significance is disputed – or both. This does not necessarily mean that they are wrong but they do need to be treated with greater care and to be subjected to more critical examination than is usually the case.

The evidence of radioactive dating

There are a number of different kinds of evidence put forward in favour of a great age for the earth; for example, the apparent expansion of the universe, the age of the oldest star clusters in our galaxy, the radioactive dating of rocks. These are all quite independent methods but all point to an age of about 15,000 million years for the universe, and about 4,500 million years for the earth. Those who believe in a young earth concentrate their attack on the reliability of radioactive dating of rocks.

This method of dating depends on the observation that radioactive elements break down at a steady rate, eventually producing stable 'daughter' elements which are not radioactive. If a rock contains a radioactive element its age can be estimated by measuring the amount of that element present, plus the amounts of its daughter elements. Advocates of a young earth criticize this dating method on two counts.

Firstly, they question the assumption that radioactive decay has always gone on at the same rate. After all, old earth advocates criticize 'young earthers' for assuming a steady rate of decrease in the strength of the earth's magnetic field. The argument cuts both ways! The response of old earth advocates is that in this case there is reasonable ground for the extrapolation. Nuclear physicists think they know why some atoms are radioactive; their theory explaining this also indicates that radioactive decay should be a steady process. Of course the theory may eventually be shown to be wrong but, at the moment, it seems valid. In addition it is pointed out that some radioactive dating techniques (the 'isochron' methods) do not depend on the assumption of regular decay; they are, rather, a way of proving that the decay is regular. Finally, it has been suggested that factors such as extreme temperatures or the level of cosmic radiation might affect the rate of radioactive decay. They clearly do not, however, since rocks from the moon and meteorites give the same ages as those from the earth.

Secondly, young earth advocates make much of the discordant results sometimes obtained from rock samples. Here they point out a real weakness in the method. For example, the daughter elements produced by the decay might get washed out of the rock by water. Most such problems, however, would result in the date obtained being too young, not too old. Also, it is possible to check whether this kind of thing has occurred and make some allowance for it. Opponents of radioactive dating are not always fair in their treatment of discordant results. It is still quite common to find them referring to the case of the dating of some lava which gave an age that was clearly too high. However, few of them point out that there is a reasonable explanation for this. The molten lava flowed over much older rock, breaking bits off it which were then trapped in the lava when it cooled. When the original samples were taken for dating this was not realized. Once it had been, it was quite easy to separate out the two types of rock and then sensible results were obtained.

Radioactive dating does have its problems but the majority of people who have studied the technique think it is unlikely to give rise to errors as great as tenfold. Even that margin of error would not be great enough to make the difference between 10,000 and 10,000 million years.

The fossil record

How is the presence of fossils to be explained if the earth is only 10,000 years old? It is not just the fact of fossils that needs explanation. They occur in distinct groups and the order in which these groups appear in the rock strata seems to be a fixed one.

The geologic column: an invention?

The arrangement of these various groups in a fixed order is called a geologic column. It can be used to give the relative dates of rock strata: group A, for instance, always appears deeper than group B, and therefore presumably occurred earlier than group B.

It is sometimes said that the geologic column was invented by evolutionists to support their theory. This is quite untrue historically. The first person to develop the geologic column was William Smith. If he were alive now he would be described as a young earth creationist. However, he lived at the end of the eighteenth century, long before evolution was an issue. He was a geological surveyor. In the course of his work he realized that certain fossils always occurred together. Moreover, in places where several undisturbed strata lay on top of one another, the different fossil groups always appeared in the same order. In any one place only part of the geologic column is found but it is not too difficult to build up the whole picture. If in one place the sequence of fossil types is ABCDE, in another is DEFGHIJ and in a third is HIJKLM, and so on, one can reasonably deduce the whole sequence. There are some places where the sequence is out of order but these can usually be explained as the result of erosion removing some layers before others were laid down over them, or as the result of major earth movements such as earthquakes.

The fossil sequence: caused by the flood?

The 'young earth, flood geology' position is so called because it maintains that the fossils and the fossil sequence are a result of Noah's flood. Advocates of this position regard the flood as a major, world-wide catastrophe (we will discuss this view of it later) and believe that the fossil sequence can be explained on the basis of three factors:

1 *Hydraulic sorting*. As they drowned in the flood it would have been the denser and more streamlined creatures which would sink to the bottom of the water first.

However, some particularly large and dense creatures, such as turtles, are never found in the lowest rock strata, while ammonoids – shell-fish which are light because their shells have buoyancy chambers full of air – are found there.

2 *Differential mobility*. The more mobile creatures would have been able to flee to higher ground and so would have been drowned last. So dinosaurs were buried before the fleeter mammals.

This does, however, leave some problems. In

the lower layers we would expect to find some fossil remains of those mammals that were sleeping, sick, injured or got trapped in their burrows as the flood waters rose. But this is not the case. We would also expect that fossilized remains of pterodactyls, which could fly, would appear in layers higher than the dinosaurs but, again, this is not the case.

3 *Ecological zoning*. Flood geologists argue that the layers of fossils, such as those in the Grand Canyon, represent different ecological zones from the sea bed to the uplands, which were inundated in succession.

The problem with this argument is that it provides no explanation for why the layers lie above one another in one place, when the uplands would have been tens or hundreds of miles away from the sea shore.

None of these three theories accounts for the distribution of plant fossils.

Flood geologists may well be able to refine their theories so that they are more convincing but much work remains to be done. We will return to some wider aspects of this subject when we discuss the flood story.

This discussion of the age of the earth and of flood geology may seem to have been rather negative. This may reflect my own prejudice. However, the advocates of a young earth and flood geology insist that their position is a scientific one and I hope that the points made about it above are the result of submitting it to scientific scrutiny. These points have all been made in more specialist scientific literature but little of it seems to have come through to the wider Christian public. The books of the young earth writers are, however, readily available in most Christian bookshops.

Evolution: the origin of life?

The young earth position is not the only anti-evolutionary one. Many of those who take the 'concordist' interpretation of Genesis 1, which we will discuss later, also reject evolution. Before turning to their view, we will look at some of the criticisms of evolution.

Life does not happen spontaneously

Darwin did not claim to have explained the origin of life, only the origin of species. For many people today, however, the theory of evolution includes the idea of life arising spontaneously on earth from non-living matter.

Some who oppose this aspect of evolutionary theory argue that Pasteur's law of biogenesis 'forbids' life arising spontaneously from non-living matter. Pasteur was fighting the idea that disease-carrying organisms grew spontaneously from dirt. He argued that they could only grow from one another. So if something, perhaps milk, is heated to kill all the disease organisms ('pasteurized') and then kept sealed so that air, which carries the organisms, cannot get at it, it will remain free of them. He proved this to be the case.

However, to say that his law of biogenesis (that disease organisms grow from each other and do not arise spontaneously from non-living matter) 'forbids' the idea that life arose spontaneously on earth is to misunderstand the nature of scientific laws, as we saw in chapter 2. They are *descriptions* of what has been observed to happen under certain conditions, they do not say what *must* happen. Moreover, Pasteur was dealing with organisms that exist today and in today's conditions. Somewhat different organisms might have been able to arise from non-living matter under the different conditions existing on the earth long ago.

Natural processes always lead to greater disorder

A second argument that is put forward against this aspect of evolutionary theory, and indeed the whole concept of evolution, appeals to the second law of thermodynamics. This law is often presented as saying that natural processes always lead to greater disorder ('increased entropy'). It is therefore argued that complex living organisms could not arise by natural processes because their structure is highly ordered (they have low entropy).

This is an over-simple application of the law. The law applies only to a 'closed system' near equilibrium. A closed system is one which cannot exchange energy with its surroundings. The earth is not closed in this sense. It constantly receives energy from the sun. Entropy can decrease on earth without violating the second law provided it increases in the sun (which it does as the sun loses energy). Also, the law only applies to processes close to equilibrium. Recently it has been shown that a system that is far from equilibrium, and able to take in energy, can spontaneously produce order. Some scientists are now investigating such systems in the hope of finding clues to how life might have arisen on earth.

If they succeed would God become redundant as creator? Not at all. It is still necessary to explain how it is that matter and the laws of thermodynamics are such that life could arise in this way. The most that can be said is that scientists may have discovered what processes God put into action when, as Genesis says, he commanded the earth to produce life.

God creates instantaneously

Some Christians are not happy with the kind of statement that speaks of God putting 'processes' into action. They argue that 'creation' has to be an instantaneous, miraculous, act. This is not, however, what the Bible actually states. Moreover, in some places God is spoken of as 'creating' something over a period of time, for example, in Isaiah 43:1,15 God is called the 'creator' of Israel, the same Hebrew word for 'create' being used as in Genesis 1. But the creation of Israel happened over a matter of centuries, from Abraham to Moses. Similarly, the creation of Adam is not presented as an instantaneous act but as a process involving two or three separate stages. This is also the case with the creation of Eve.

Having said all that, it must be added that in fact scientists have not got very far in their attempts to explain how life might have arisen spontaneously on earth. It used to be thought that the atmosphere on the early earth contained hydrogen, methane, ammonia, nitrogen and water. It has been shown that when electrical sparks (lightning?) are put through such a mixture amino-acids, the building blocks of the proteins needed for life, are produced. However, geologists now believe that the atmosphere on the early earth was quite different from this and was made up of different gases (carbon dioxide, water and a little oxygen) which would not produce amino-acids.

It has also been pointed out that the early earth would have lacked the protective atmosphere it now has. As a result the intensity of cosmic rays and ultra-violet light reaching the surface would have been enough to destroy the chemical compounds that are the building blocks of living organisms.

Some scientists are so sceptical of the possibility of life being able to arise on earth that they have suggested that it reached earth from outer space, perhaps via meteorites (see F Hoyle and N Wickramasinghe, *Evolution from Space*).

My own conclusion is that claims that life could, or must, have arisen spontaneously on earth are still no more than statements of faith in a hypothesis that has very little scientific evidence to support it.

Evolution: the origin of species?

The theory of evolution is far too big a topic to discuss at length in this book. All we can do is mention briefly a few of the major objections to it and the responses to them.

Missing links in the fossil record

One of the most telling areas of attack on evolution has been the fossil evidence. Darwin admitted that the fossil evidence which, to some extent, seemed to support his theory, also posed problems for it. He was worried about the absence of transitional forms between the separate species, genera and so on. He was also worried by the sudden appearance of the main divisions of animals in the earliest rocks. He hoped that as the study of fossils advanced the problems would disappear. They have not. A recent defender of evolution, M Ridley, says concerning the 'missing links', 'a few dozen could be listed. But the most striking thing about them is their rarity' (*The Problems of Evolution*, p 11).

Some evolutionists have responded to this problem by proposing modified forms of the theory. For example, it has been argued that evolution may proceed best in small groups of creatures which are under ecological stress. In a small group genetic mutations (changes in the hereditary material passed from parents to offspring) are more likely to be preserved and spread due to inbreeding. If the group is under stress (eg prey to a fast-running killer) any advantageous change (eg ability to run faster, better camouflage) would have immediate effect and so be even more rapidly established. So, it is argued, evolution occurred in situations where few transitional forms would be left, because it involved few creatures and happened in rapid (geologically speaking) spurts. This suggestion may be correct but it makes evolution almost untestable, at least by means of the fossils.

Opponents of evolution have sometimes pointed to fossils that are out of place as a way of trying to discredit the fossil evidence. The best known example of this has been the so-called man tracks amongst dinosaur foot prints in the Paluxy River bed in Texas. However, J Morris, one of the popularisers of this evidence, has now, to his credit, admitted that the 'human' tracks are either badly formed dinosaur foot prints or simply the result of rock erosion.

Small changes, not large ones
Most anti-evolutionists accept that small changes do occur and even that new species can arise as a result of genetic mutations and natural selection. What they do not accept is that this could lead to major changes. Here they make two main points. Firstly, we have no evidence that major changes have happened (which is true if the fossil evidence is discounted as too debatable). Secondly, it is inconceivable that a major organ could undergo change (eg a hand becoming a wing) without passing through a stage in which it would be a major disadvantage to the creature concerned.

Evolutionists admit the first point but add that this is inevitably the case since major changes take a long time. Again, the theory becomes untestable. They reply to the second by saying that the problem lies in their opponents' understanding and imagination. Evolutionists conceive of such a change taking place by a series of very small steps, each change either making no difference or giving a small advantage to the creature. Some evolutionists lay a lot of stress on what they call 'neutral mutations', which have little or no effect. These, they argue, can build up until some change in the environment results in them producing an important advantage. One of the difficulties for the non-expert is that modern genetics is a highly mathematical discipline which it is not easy to understand.

Natural selection seems cruel and wasteful

Another argument against evolution is not a scientific one but is moral and theological. It is argued that the process of natural selection is cruel and wasteful and is unworthy of a good God. Christian evolutionists agree that there is no simple answer to this problem, any more than there is a simple answer to the question why God allows the existence of evil and seems to be slow in eradicating it. However, they do suggest two lines of argument that go some way towards dealing with the problem.

They point out that whether something is wasteful or not depends on the end product of a process. Simply to whittle away at a piece of wood until nothing is left but wood shavings might well be considered wasteful. However if the end product was a pile of wood shavings and also a beautifully carved Welsh love-spoon, most people would not consider that the wood had been wasted, even if most of it had ended up as shavings. God is the craftsman of the universe and we must allow him to decide what is the best way to produce the end result he desires and whether or not it is wasteful.

Secondly, they argue that there is often more sentiment than real thought involved in this argument. It is certainly wrong for humans to abuse animals (and plants), cause them unnecessary suffering or kill them wantonly. This is because we are moral beings answerable to God for the way we treat his creation, of which he has made us stewards. As far as we know, animals have no moral sense and so we cannot apply moral categories to the way they treat each other. Also, since we do not know what goes on in the minds of prey and predator or of an injured animal, it is not clear how or whether terms such as 'cruelty' or 'suffering' can be used of them. We may be transferring our reactions to them illegitimately.

G F Wright, who was an original 'fundamentalist' in the sense that he contributed to the pamphlets *The Fundamentals* from which the term derives, said this about evolution (see C A Russell, *Cross-Currents*, p 163),

> 'If only the evolutionists would incorporate into their system the sweetness of the Calvinistic doctrine of Divine Sovereignty, the church would make no objection to their speculation.'

He was willing to accept the idea of evolution as a God-directed process.

A lot more could be said both for and against the theory of evolution. Later we will look at the debate over the possible evolutionary origin of the human race. It ought to be clear from what we have said that the question of evolution is not easily resolved, either scientifically or theologically. There is plenty of room for legitimate disagreement about it among Christians.

CHAPTER 5
Beginnings: Other Approaches

Concordist approaches to Genesis 1:1–2:3

A number of suggestions have been made about how Genesis 1 might be interpreted in a way that is in accord with the findings of modern science. These have been concerned mainly with the evidence for the great age of the earth and the existence of the fossils, rather than with the theory of evolution. They have been labelled 'concordist' interpretations of Genesis 1. Many, if not most, concordists have rejected evolution. We will deal briefly with only three examples of this kind of approach.

A gap in creative activity

The 'gap' or 'restitution' theory was first put forward at the end of the eighteenth century. It was popularized by Scofield when he adopted it in his *Reference Bible*. According to this theory Genesis

1:1 refers to the original creation of the earth. The earth then suffered ruin and destruction as a result of the rebellion and fall of Lucifer and some of the angels. To accord with this Genesis 1:2 has to be translated, 'The earth *became* formless and void.' The rest of the chapter can then be read as the restitution of the earth by God in six literal days. All but the most recent rock strata and all the fossils are relegated to the original, ruined, creation.

There are at least two major problems with this theory.

For one thing, it rests a major piece of teaching on a very rare meaning for the form of the Hebrew verb 'to be' which is used in Genesis 1:2.

Secondly, there is no clear statement elsewhere in the Bible that the fall of the angels had a ruinous effect on the earth. Attempts to find a hint of it in Isaiah 24:1 and Jeremiah 4:23–26 depend on what most scholars would see as very dubious interpretations.

'The 'days' were 'ages'

A number of 'age-day' interpretations of Genesis 1 have been proposed. Their common factor is that the 'days' of creation are taken figuratively, representing successive ages – unspecified periods of many millions of years each. There has been a great deal written about whether or not the Hebrew word for 'day' (*yōm*) can be used in a non-literal way. Much of this is beside the point. It is not just the word 'day' that has to be considered. In its strongest form the age-day interpretation takes the whole week of Genesis 1 to be a metaphorical week, a form of picture language. The creative activity of God over millions of years is pictured as if it were the activity of a normal working week. Some argue that the metaphorical nature of the language is indicated by what is said of the seventh day. There is no mention of 'evening and morning', implying that it has still not ended. This non-literal view of the seventh day also seems required by what Jesus says in John 5:17, which depends for its force on the assumption that we are still in the 'sabbath' of creation week. Exodus 20:11 presents no problem to this interpretation. It says no more than that the pattern of the human week is to be based on the pattern of the divine week of seven creative ages.

Supporters of the age-day view point out that there is a general agreement between the order of the creative acts and the geological and fossil evidence, though the correspondence is not exact. For example trees appear before the marine creatures, and birds before insects (if they are included in verse 25), contrary to the fossil evidence. Above all, of course, evening and morning appear before the sun and moon. The last point is often met by saying that the account describes things as they would have appeared to someone on the earth. We are to understand that the sun, moon and stars were created when light was created. They only became visible from the surface of the earth when the clouds which probably shrouded the earth for much of its history, cleared – perhaps partly due to the effect of plants on the composition of the atmosphere. Other difficulties are explained as the result of the account being concise and therefore partly topical. For instance, all the plants are mentioned together at the time when plants were first created. Critics of this interpretation claim that these arguments seem more like evasions of the problem than explanations of them.

Days of revelation

A third type of interpretation argues that the days of Genesis 1 are literal days but they are not the days when God carried out the acts of creation. They are 'revelatory days' when he revealed his work of creation to the author of Genesis. How, it is argued, could any human come to know about God's creative activity when no one was there until it was nearly over? The answer is: only if God revealed it to someone. Genesis 1 gives a (brief) record of the process of *revelation*, which was spread over six literal days. The order of the creative acts is either said to be topical or (in order to relate it to the fossils) a mixture of chronological and topical.

Probably the greatest weakness of this view is that it is not at all clear that Genesis 1 is meant to be read as the account of a process of revelation, rather than the process of creation.

Neither the age-day nor the revelatory-day interpretation is necessarily either pro- or anti-evolution. They leave open the question of how God brought living things into being out of the earth and the waters.

A literary-cultural approach to Genesis 1:1–2:3

When discussing the rules that should guide our interpretation of the Bible we saw that it is very important to understand what kind of literature we are dealing with. Is it poetry or prose? If it is prose, what kind of prose is it? The final approach to Genesis 1 that we shall deal with takes these questions as its starting point. It does not simply assume that Genesis 1 is literal prose but asks what evidence there is in the passage itself to help us see what kind of literature it is.

In our discussion of the age-day approach we saw that it seems necessary to take the seventh day of creation in a non-literal way. Might this be an indication that we should do the same with the others? If so, are there other similar indications? From the early Christian centuries onwards some commentators on the chapter have found evidence for a non-literal reading of it in the fact that it seems to have a structure that makes excellent logical sense but not such good chronological sense. This is set out in diagram 1. When first created the earth is said to be shapeless and empty. The first three days deal with its shape and the second three with filling it up with creatures suitable to its different parts. The two series of days parallel one another beautifully. The whole structure of the passage reflects and speaks of the order, harmony and beauty of God's creation (the word 'good' in Hebrew has as one of its senses 'beautiful'). God is presented as a good craftsman and so perhaps the 'week' here is meant to be no more than a figure of speech, which comes naturally to mind when speaking of the work of a craftsman. It is suggested, then, that the purpose of the passage is to speak of the nature of God's creative activity and its outcome, not the details of how he went about it. Hence to ask of it the 'How?' questions which interest modern science is to ask the wrong kind of question, and to get a wrong answer.

Diagram 1 – The structure of Genesis 1:1–2:3

The earth was

shapeless and	**empty**
Day 1 The separation of light and darkness.	Day 4 The creation of the lights to rule the day and the night.
Day 2 The separation of the waters to form the sky and the sea.	*Day 5* The creation of the birds and fish to fill the sky and sea.
Day 3 The separation of the sea from the dry land and creation of plants.	*Day 6* The creation of the animals and humans to fill the land and eat the plants.

Day 7

The heavens and the earth were finished and God rested.

Understanding the literature

It is often said that Genesis 1 is not Hebrew poetry. This is true in the strict sense. However, neither is it simple prose. It has some of the features of Hebrew poetry, such as repetition of phrases, parallelism, carefully balanced phraseology. Moreover, even in English translation there is a rhythmic quality about it that is not there in simple prose. This arises because many words and phrases in the passage are repeated three, seven, or ten times. Here is a list of some of them (these are not always clear in English translations):

Phrases that occur ten times:

- 'God said'

(three times concerning man, seven times concerning other things);

- creative commands

(three times 'Let there be . . .' and seven times 'Let');

- 'to make';
- 'according to their kind'.

Phrases that occur seven times:

- 'and it was so';
- 'and God saw that it was good'.

Three times it is said that:

- God blessed.
- God created.
- God created men and women.

- 'Earth' and 'God' are each mentioned twenty-one times, that is, three times seven.
- The introduction (1:1–2) contains twenty-one words in Hebrew (three times seven), and the conclusion (2:1–3) contains thirty-five words (five time seven).

All this, it is argued, points to an author who is primarily concerned with symbolism (in this case the symbolism of numbers) and so perhaps not concerned (or inspired) to give an exact chronological account.

Understanding the cultural setting

To this literary argument for taking the passage in a non-literal way is added a cultural argument. This arises from another of the rules of interpretation that we considered: the need to understand what it would have meant to the original writer and readers. Study of the ideas of creation that were around in the near east in Old Testament times throws much light on Genesis 1. We will look at this in more detail later but will give a couple of examples now.

Firstly, why are the sun and moon not called by their names, but only referred to as 'lights'? There are perfectly good, common words for sun and moon in Hebrew.

The probable answer is that in the Semitic languages, of which Hebrew is one, the words 'sun' and 'moon' are also the names of gods. The peoples around the Hebrews worshipped the heavenly bodies as gods and goddesses. Genesis 1:14–19 is an attack on all such thinking. The heavenly bodies are simply 'lights' (just like great big oil lamps!) created by the God of Israel to serve humans (not for humans to serve!) as calendar markers.

Secondly, the Hebrew verb *bārā'* ('to create'), which in the Old Testament is used only of God's creative activity, occurs three times in the story, in verses 1, 21 and 27. It seems understandable that it should be used in the initial statement abut God's creative work in verse 1 and of the final act (the creation of humans) in verse 27. But why is it used in verse 21?

The only convincing answer has to do with the significance of sea monsters in one of the creation stories of Babylon (and probably Canaan too). Here the creator god has to subdue the forces of chaos, depicted as sea monsters, before creating the heavens and the earth. Genesis 1 rejects this by stressing that the sea monsters are just part of God's creation. He did not have to fight and subdue them, he made them!

It is argued that the more closely one looks at Genesis 1 in the light of the religious ideas with which the Hebrews had to do battle, the clearer it is that the meaning of the passage is essentially theological, not historical or scientific. It deals with the questions which theology asks, not those which science asks.

Those theological questions are just as relevant today as they were 3,000 years ago. They are more important than the scientific questions since they go to the heart of the meaning and purpose of the universe in a way that science cannot.

There is a further consideration. If a literal interpretation of the passage runs into problems with the evidence concerning the age of the earth, the fossils and so on, it may be because the nature of the literature and language has been misunderstood. The evidence of the two 'books' of God's revelation in nature and Scripture ought not to be at cross-purposes.

There are two main criticisms of this literary-cultural approach. Firstly, literalists regard it as too subtle. They argue that their reading of Genesis 1 is much simpler and more obvious. However, what is simple and obvious depends on the way you approach something. The literalists are open to the charge of being more concerned with what is simple and obvious to them, than with what would have been simple and obvious to the first readers or hearers of Genesis 1:1–2:3. The real issue is how well the rules of interpretation are being applied.

The second criticism of the literary-cultural approach is that it largely ignores the questions raised by science. The answer given to this is that the problem lies in the exaggerated importance our modern culture gives to science and scientific truth. The questions dealt with by Genesis are in fact the more relevant ones.

A pause for thought

It is too early in our study to come to definite conclusions about the different approaches to Genesis 1. The literal and literary-cultural approaches can also be applied to the rest of Genesis 1–11. Whether or not they make good sense there too will obviously influence what we think of their application to chapter 1.

Our study of Genesis 1:1–2:3 has, however, highlighted three issues.

Firstly, the method of interpretation is the most fundamental issue. It seems that the literal approach is too simplistic because it does not take all the rules of good interpretation seriously enough. It *assumes* that Genesis 1:1–2:3 is to be read as simple prose and as addressed directly to the concerns of twentieth-century people. Those who adopt it do not take the time and effort needed to look at the passage through the eyes of the ancient Israelites to whom it was first addressed. As a result the light that our knowledge of the literature and culture of the ancient near east can throw on how we should understand it is ignored. The literary-cultural approach seems to be a sounder method of interpretation and makes good sense of the passage.

The second issue is the age of the earth. The literalistic interpretation of Genesis comes into head-on conflict with the age of the earth as scientists have determined it by a number of independent methods – all of which produce an answer of several thousand million years. It is my experience that most Christian geologists find the 'scientific' arguments for a young earth scientifically unsound. This is true even of those who, like Davis Young (see his book *Christianity and the Age of the Earth*), are anti-evolution.

Thirdly, the theory of evolution is not compatible with a literal interpretation of Genesis 1. It seems that most Christians involved in the 'life sciences' are unconvinced by the arguments against evolution, though they accept that they do raise some searching questions about it. The attempts to use the flood to explain the fossil evidence do not seem very satisfactory. Apart from the literal interpretation of Genesis, there is no strong theological reason for denying the possibility that God used an evolutionary process to bring into existence the life forms he wanted.

The literary-cultural approach is not directly affected by the scientific arguments about the age of the earth and evolution. This is because it leads to the conclusion that the message of Genesis 1:1–2:3 is theological (we will look at what it says in some detail later). It concentrates on the nature of God and the world he created, and his purposes in creating it. The question of *how* he did it is left open.

This should not surprise us in view of what we have seen earlier about the complementary nature of scientific and religious truth. The 'how?' questions are the legitimate concern of scientists. We have seen that their answers should not be rejected lightly. If they do conflict with our understanding of what the Bible says, then we should think seriously about the soundness of our method of interpretation as well as examining the soundness of the scientific claims. The 'rules of interpretation' we have discussed were not drawn up with the problems of Genesis in mind. They are rules which have arisen as a result of applying the results of the study of literature in general to the study of the Bible. The literary-cultural approach to Genesis seems to apply them more carefully and consistently than the literalistic approach does, and this is a decisive point in its favour.

CHAPTER 6
Puzzles in Genesis 2–5

> ‘[4]This is the account of the heavens and the earth when they were created.
>
> When the Lord God made the earth and the heavens, [5]no shrub of the field had yet appeared on the earth and no plant of the field had yet sprung up; the Lord God had not sent rain on the earth and there was no man to work the ground, [6]but streams came up from the earth and watered the whole surface of the ground. [7]And the Lord God formed man from the dust of the ground and breathed into his nostrils the breath of life, and man became a living being.
>
> [8]Now the Lord God had planted a garden in the east, in Eden; and there he put the man he had formed. [9]And the Lord God made all kinds of trees grow out of the ground – trees that were pleasing to the eye and good for food. In the middle of the garden were the tree of life and the tree of the knowledge of good and evil.’ (Genesis 2:4–9)

Some people find these verses puzzling, coming after the creation story in chapter 1. They read a bit like the beginning of another, different creation story.

A contradictory account?

According to some Old Testament scholars Genesis 2:4–25 contains a second creation story which contradicts that of Genesis 1:1–2:3. In chapter 2, they say, man is created before the plants and animals. Also 2:5 seems to show the early earth as an arid desert, not the watery chaos of 1:2. What can we say about this?

Firstly, when we looked at the 'rules of interpretation' we saw that if the Bible is inspired by God, who is truth, we would not expect it to contradict itself. This encourages us to look for ways of harmonizing apparent contradictions, provided this can be done without twisting Scripture.

Secondly, even if this were not the case, it would be strange if the author of Genesis simply put two contradictory accounts of creation side-by-side.

Bearing these two points in mind, it makes good sense to see chapter 1 as a panoramic view of God's creative work, with chapter 2 then focussing in on the climactic work, the creation of human beings. Verses 5 and 6 of chapter 2 can be taken as referring to the state of things in the area where the garden of Eden came into being – arid, but fertile if properly irrigated. The mention of plants being created refers only to the garden of Eden and need not imply that plants did not already exist elsewhere.

Finally, the Hebrew verb used in verse 19 allows it to mean, 'Now the Lord God *had* formed out of the ground all the beasts of the field . . .' (as in the NIV), referring back to an earlier act of creation.

The location of Eden

> ‘[10]A river watering the garden flowed from Eden,
> and from there it divided; it had four headstreams.
> [11]The name of the first is the Pishon; it winds
> through the entire land of Havilah, where there is
> gold. [12](The gold of that land is good; aromatic resin
> and onyx are also there.) [13]The name of the second
> river is the Gihon; it winds through the entire land
> of Cush. [14]The name of the third river is the Tigris;
> it runs along the east side of Asshur. And the fourth
> river is the Euphrates.’ (Genesis 2:10–14)

The location of the garden of Eden, as indicated by these verses, is a matter for debate. There are two main views.

Some think that the description points to a place at the head of the Persian Gulf, where the Tigris and Euphrates met and formed a delta. This view is influenced partly by the identification of Havilah with Arabia, suggested by Genesis 25:18: ‘[Ishmael's] descendants settled in the area from Havilah to Shur, near the border of Egypt, as you go towards Asshur.’ Also, in Babylonian literature paradise is thought of as located in the Persian Gulf. There is some evidence to link the Babylonian paradise with the island of Bahrein.

The other view places Eden in the upland plateaux of what is now castern Turkey, where the Tigris and Euphrates rise. The other two rivers are then sometimes identified with the Araxes (flowing into the Caspian Sea) and Halys (flowing into the Black Sea). In ancient times gold was found in some of the rivers in the area between the Caspian and Black Seas. The story of Jason's golden fleece relates to this region. The location of Havilah is by no means definitely Arabia. Cush in the Old Testament usually clearly refers to Ethiopia but this cannot be the case in Genesis 2. In Genesis 10:6–10 Cush may mean the Kassite people who lived in western Iran in antiquity. This Cush is also linked with Havilah (10:7), which may therefore have been in the same kind of region.

Both of the locations suggested for Eden had an arid climate in ancient times and we cannot choose between them simply on the basis of Genesis 2:10–14. We will look at this again later.

Interpreting Genesis 2 and 3

Interpretations of Genesis 2 and 3 come in two varieties – the 'literal' and the 'literary-cultural'. Those who adopt a 'concordist' approach for Genesis 1 are divided over how to interpret chapters 2 and 3.

The literal approach

The literal approach to interpretation may seem quite simple and straightforward here, but it does have problems. For instance, are we really to take 2:7 literally, with God forming a dust pile into human form and breathing into it? '. . . the Lord God formed man from the dust of the ground and breathed into his nostrils the breath of life, and man became a living being.' Surely the 'breathing' at least must be metaphorical. God does not have lungs and nostrils as we do.

If we take 2:21–22 literally we must assume that God behaved as a modern surgeon carrying out an operation: 'So the Lord God caused the man to fall into a deep sleep; and while he was sleeping, he took one of the man's ribs and closed up the place with flesh. Then the Lord God made a woman from the rib he had taken out of the man, and he brought her to the man.'

There are more problems as we go on. Why was Cain afraid of being killed (4:14)? Who would there be to kill him? And from where did he get his wife? The obvious, (literal?) reading of 4:14 seems to show that there were a lot of other humans around: 'I will be a restless wanderer on the earth, and whoever finds me will kill me.'

We cannot rule out a literal understanding of these passages but it does seem reasonable to at least consider whether they are meant to be taken figuratively.

The literary-cultural approach

Starting with these clues, the literary-cultural approach looks for other evidence that Genesis 2 and 3 might be intended more as a figurative account than as a simple historical one. There is quite a lot of such evidence. To begin with, the content of Genesis 2–3 is structured in a symmetrical way similar to that of Genesis 1, though it is not so obvious (see diagram 2).

The story contains a number of word-plays. For instance the word used for pain in 3:16 is not the usual Hebrew one for the pain of childbirth. It seems to have been chosen because it sounds like the Hebrew word for 'tree' (a bit like 'trauma' and 'tree' in English). Similarly, the Hebrew words for 'naked', 'crafty' and 'curse' sound very alike.

In the book of Revelation the serpent (12:15) and the tree of life (22:2) are clearly used in a symbolic, non-literal way. Might that be the case in Genesis, too? It is also pointed out that, in the literature of the ancient near east, paradise, the serpent and the tree of life are common religious symbols.

To say that Genesis 2 and 3 give a figurative, symbolic, account is not to say that it is unhistorical. Real historical events can be described in a symbolic way. To describe something symbolically can actually be a powerful way of bringing out its significance. Revelation 12:1–6 describes forcefully – and symbolically – how the Messiah came from the people of God in the face of Satan's opposition.

When an historical event is described in a non-literal, symbolic way we cannot get behind the symbolic language to reconstruct a simple historical account of the events to which it refers unless we have other evidence to help us. If Revelation 12:1–6 were the only account we had of Christ's coming we could not reconstruct the historical event. But, in fact, we do have the accounts in the Gospels which give us the historical details. Genesis 2–3 does seem to refer to a definite historical event because of the geographical setting given to it, the genealogies which follow it and give it a chronological setting and the use made of the story in the New Testament, especially in Romans 5. However, if it is written in symbolic language we have to be very cautious in what we try to say about this event. Even so, as we shall see, it is possible to make some suggestions about it with the help of other evidence. As a result, the literary-cultural approach makes good sense of Genesis 2–3. Since it also takes seriously the clearly symbolic language of the story, it seems more satisfactory than the literal approach.

Diagram 2 – The Structure of Genesis 2 and 3

2: 4–6. Introduction

2: 7–17. Adam created and placed in Eden.	3:20–24. Adam and Eve driven out of Eden.
2: 18–25. Relationships established between: mankind and the animals, man and woman.	3: 14–19. The effect on the relationships between: man and woman, mankind and nature.
3: 1–5. The serpent's question.	3: 8–13. God's question.

3: 6–7. Eve and Adam eat the forbidden fruit.

The first people

Who was Adam?

One possible reconstruction of the historical background to Genesis 2 and 3 has been suggested in a book entitled *Who Was Adam?* by a biblical scholar and anthropologist, Canon E K V Pearce.

He starts with the picture the Bible gives us of Adam and his family's way of life both before and after they left Eden. They are shown tilling the soil and herding animals. There is the implication that they used stone tools since one of their descendants, Tubal-Cain, seems to have been the first person to use metal: '. . . Tubal-Cain, who forged all kinds of tools out of bronze and iron' (Genesis 4:22). In scientific terms, Adam's way of life would be described as 'Neolithic' or New Stone Age. In the Old Stone Age food was obtained by hunting, and by gathering wild plants, not by farming. The Bronze Age followed the Neolithic Age.

Pearce points out that the Neolithic culture arose in the uplands of Turkey which, as we saw, is one possible site for Eden. From there it spread to Europe, Asia and the Middle East. The beginning of the Neolithic Age is usually dated around 8000 BC. Interestingly, Cain is said to have built a city (4:17) and archeologists have found Neolithic cities. One of the earliest is Çatal Hüyük in upland Turkey.

If Pearce's suggestion is accepted, and it cannot be considered more than a plausible theory, it still leaves unanswered the questions of exactly what happened in Eden and how Adam and his descendants are to be related to the fossil creatures that are supposed to be the ancestors of modern human beings. We must now see what can be said about this, always remembering that a good deal of guess-work is involved.

Who was Cain's wife?

Those who reject the theory of evolution, whether on the basis of a literal interpretation of Genesis 1–2 or some other grounds, regard the creation of Adam and Eve as a special act of God. They see the so-called 'fossil men' as ape-like creatures which were in no way human. Cain's wife, then, has to be one of his sisters, and his fear expressed in 4:14 was a fear of future relatives of his, not yet born.

Christians who accept evolution argue that God used that process to bring into being a physical body appropriate for the spiritual nature made in God's image – human nature. They point out that the image of God referred to in Genesis 1:27 cannot be our physical appearance: 'So God created man in his own image, in the image of God he created him; male and female he created them.' God is spirit and does not have a physical body. Genesis 2:7 is taken as saying in picture language that we are made partly of dust, just like the animals, but also have a spiritual nature which survives our physical death and the return of our body to the dust: 'the Lord God formed the man from the dust of the ground and breathed into his nostrils the breath of life, and the man became a living being.' It is this spiritual nature which makes us human beings and not just animals. Since we do not really understand the relationship between the physical and non-physical aspects of our being (the body-mind and body-soul relationships have been much debated by philosophers and theologians down through the centuries) we cannot say how God brought the two into union. The moment he did this, the first humans were created.

The fossil evidence is of little relevance here. Fossils, by their nature, can be classified only on the basis of their physical features – whether the creature walked upright, its brain size and so on. There is no reason why possession of the image of God, a spiritual quality, should be related to any change in physical form.

Anthropologists try to classify the fossil creatures using the evidence of how they lived; for instance, the use of tools. However, some animals make use of sticks and stones as primitive tools and so this is not a sure test of humanness. Even evidence of deliberate burial of the dead does not prove the existence of a god-consciousness. In fact the earliest clear evidence of creatures worshipping God seems to be the existence of religious sanctuaries, found in the Neolithic city of Çatal Hüyük.

Whatever else may be in dispute, biologists and anthropologists agree that all the existing races of human beings belong to one single, unified species, which they call *Homo Sapiens Sapiens*. They believe that this species originated at least 50,000 years ago.

Some Christian evolutionists argue that when Adam and Eve received the image of God – human nature – there would have been many other creatures just like them physically. These too would have been able to receive human nature. Maybe, they suggest, after the fall God conferred (fallen) human nature on all those who shared Adam and Eve's physical nature. This would explain both Cain's fear and where his wife came from. Does this idea, however, fit with other biblical statements about human origins?

On examination, none of the key biblical passages clearly rules out this idea. Romans 5:12–21 stresses a single sinful act as the source of human sinfulness but does not say how sin spread to all humans from that act. 1 Corinthians 15:45–48 calls Adam 'the first man' and says that all humans since share his nature, but there is nothing in the evolutionists' view to contradict this since nothing is said of how this nature was passed on. Paul's statement in Acts 17:26 that 'From one man [God] made every nation of men' could mean this, but since Adam is not mentioned in the Greek text (the Greek just says 'one', not even 'one man') it could simply be a general way of stressing the unity of the human race. Finally, there is Genesis 3:20, where we are told that Adam named his wife Eve 'because she was the mother of all the living'. This is often assumed to say that she is the physical ancestor of all humans. However, Christian evolutionists argue that that is not what it actually says. It speaks of 'all the living'. This is significant just after the sin which has led to the sentence of death on the human race and the hint of salvation through the seed of the woman. 'The living' here may then refer to those who will find life through the coming saviour. These interpretations of Acts 17:26 and Genesis 3:20 are debatable but not impossible.

This discussion of the biblical evidence would seem to indicate that acceptance of evolution as the process that God used to bring human beings into existence does not lead to any necessary conflict with the Bible. If that is the case, we are left to decide whether or not to accept the theory of evolution on the basis of the scientific evidence.

Note on radiocarbon dating

The dating of the most recent fossils, including those that are supposed to be human, is done using a radioactive form of carbon called carbon–14 (C–14). This method can only be applied to the remains of living things and so cannot be used to date rocks. In addition the relatively rapid rate at which C–14 breaks down means that it cannot be used to date things more than about 40,000 years old. For this reason radiocarbon dating is not relevant when discussing the age of the earth. Its major importance lies in its use for dating supposedly human fossils. The reliability of this dating technique has been especially strongly attacked by the 'young earth, flood geology' school.

It is certainly the most inaccurate of the radioactive dating techniques. The reason for this is well known. Living creatures absorb C–14 from the air while alive. When they die this stops and the amount of C–14 in their remains decays according to the normal law of radioactive decay. The problem is that the C–14 in the air is produced by the nitrogen molecules in the air being bombarded by cosmic rays. The intensity of this bombardment varies and so does the concentration of C–14 as a result. This makes it difficult to be sure exactly how much C–14 there was in a fossil when the creature that produced it died. There are ways around this difficulty but it is a major reason for the inaccuracy in this dating method. Another problem is that the original determination of the rate at which C–14 breaks down was slightly wrong (by about three per cent) and so the initial dates determined by this method have had to be corrected.

It is possible to cross-check C–14 dates back to about 5000 BC by counting the tree rings of some very old, slow growing trees, such as the bristle-cone pines of North America. These cross-checks show that the dates are reasonably reliable and certainly by no means as wildly inaccurate as some critics claim.

The fall and its effects

This brings us to the matter of the disobedience of Adam and Eve (usually referred to as 'the fall') and its effects on creation.

The fall, sin and death

Many Christians assume that all death, human and non-human, is a result of the fall. This raises a practical problem. How would the earth support an ever-growing population of creatures if there were no death (think of the rabbit population alone!)?

In addition, the assumption that death for all creatures resulted from the fall is, I believe, based on a misreading of the Bible. The discovery of fossils led to the question of death and the fall being discussed in the nineteenth century long before the theory of evolution came on the scene.

Dr J Orr, a noted Scottish evangelical theologian and, like G F Wright one of the original 'fundamentalists', summed up the result of a century of debate when he wrote,

> 'There is not a word in the Bible to indicate that in its view death entered the animal world as a consequence of the sin of man.' (*The Christian View of God and the World*, p 197.)

On the contrary, it would seem that the Bible speaks of death as a penalty for sin only in relation to men and women.

It is also important to think about what the Bible means by death. God said to Adam that he was not to eat the fruit of the tree of the knowledge of good and evil because 'when (literally, on the day that) you eat of it you will surely die'. But they did not die immediately. Adam lived to be 930! Was God bluffing, as the serpent suggested (3:4)? No. The answer lies in the difference between the biblical view of death and ours. We tend to think of it in purely physical terms, as the moment when our physical existence ends. However, the various biblical references to death make most sense when death is seen as a spiritual power, not just an event at the end of life. It is a power which weakens and diminishes life, eventually leading to its end. One falls into the power of death when cut off from God, the source of life (see Deuteronomy 30:15–20). This non-physical meaning of death is clearly meant in John 8:51: 'I tell you the truth, if a man keeps my word, he will never see death.' In this sense Adam and Eve began to experience death as soon as they were expelled from Eden, where they had lived in close communion with God.

What is said of the tree of life in Genesis 2 and 3, especially 3:22, implies that Adam and Eve were not naturally immortal: 'And the Lord God said, "The man has now become like one of us, knowing good and evil. He must not be allowed to reach out his hand and take from the tree of life and eat, and live for ever." ' What their physical destiny would have been if they had not sinned we cannot say. Maybe their life on this earth would have ended the way Enoch's seems to have, being taken into the presence of God without dying physically (Genesis 5:24).

This discussion indicates that the death which results from sin is not to be equated simply with physical death, and that the Bible presents it as a penalty due to humans alone. There is nothing in the Bible to say that the death of animals is in itself an evil, or that it did not happen before the fall, or would not have happened had there been no fall. Also, there is no reason to attribute moral value to the purely physical process of degeneration which leads to animal death. As we have seen earlier, moral values only come into play when dealing with moral beings, humans.

Nature and the fall

> '14 So the Lord God said to the serpent, "Because you have done this,
>
> Cursed are you above all the livestock
> and all the wild animals!
> You will crawl on your belly

and you will eat dust
all the days of your life.
[15]And I will put enmity
between you and the woman,
and between your offspring and hers;
he will crush your head,
and you will strike his heel."
[16]To the woman he said,
"I will greatly increase your pains in childbearing;
with pain you will give birth to children.
Your desire will be for your husband,
and he will rule over you."
[17]To Adam he said, "Because you listened to your wife and ate from the tree about which I commanded you, 'You must not eat of it,'
"Cursed is the ground because of you;
through painful toil you will eat of it
all the days of your life.
[18]It will produce thorns and thistles for you,
and you will eat the plants of the field.
[19]By the sweat of your brow
you will eat your food
until you return to the ground,
since from it you were taken;
for dust you are
and to dust you will return." ' (Genesis 3:14–19)

What, apart from death for humans, has been the effect of the fall? The simple answer to this is that we do not really know. Paul in Romans 8:18–23 says that the entry of sin into the world has had an effect that is not restricted to human death. However, the verses in Genesis 3:14–19 are not very detailed. In addition, we are told so little about life in Eden before the fall that if we try to say much about the wider effects of the fall we end up in unfounded and fruitless speculation.

One point worth stressing is that the emphasis in these verses is not on changes in *things* (with the exception of the serpent, which is a symbol of all that is opposed to God), but on changes in *relationships*. The relationship between human beings and their creator is ruptured. As a result of this a person's relationship with himself or herself is damaged (there is guilt and shame). People can no longer get on together in harmony (Adam blames Eve). The previously harmonious relationship between humans and the rest of creation is lost.

We cannot say what kind of changes, if any, this made to non-human nature. The statement about 'thorns and thistles' in 3:18 need not mean that they had not existed before but only that our ability to cultivate the plants we want has been impaired by the fall and the loss of a proper *rapport* with nature. It is sometimes assumed that such things as earthquakes and storms are a result of the fall. But this would require a major change in the laws of nature (which, of course, God is free to change) and seems contrary to the evidence of geology. Maybe the result of the fall is not that these things happen but that we lack the power which Jesus, the perfect human being, had to deal with nature.

Evolution and the fall

It is sometimes said, both by evolutionists and their opponents, that evolution means humans have gradually become better morally. But this commits the logical mistake which we discussed in chapter 1 of trying to make statements of moral value on a scientific basis.

As a biological theory, as distinct from a philosophical position, evolution says no more or less than that *Homo Sapiens Sapiens* has become gradually more complex in certain ways and better adapted physically to life on earth. This says nothing about our moral progress or decline. Indeed, as we have seen, science cannot say anything about the origin or basis of morality. Some have tried to find a basis for it in natural instincts. The problem, as always, is that it is necessary to go outside of science to evaluate these. For example some 'evolutionary moralists' emphasize aggression, others emphasize co-operativeness. Both groups can make a case for these being essential for survival in an evolutionary framework! The truth is that both these traits can be used for good or evil. Aggression can be directed to fight against what is evil. People can co-operate with one another against God, as we shall see in Genesis 11.

The genealogies

Before leaving Genesis 2–5 we need to say something about the genealogies in chapters 4–5 and elsewhere in Genesis 1–11. We have seen that literalists are happy to accept that these may be selective and incomplete and that, if so, there is no problem about dating Adam to 8000 or 10,000 BC. But should we take the numbers literally?

All the ages given in the standard Hebrew Bible (there are differences in the Samaritan and Greek versions) are multiples of five, with either seven or fourteen added occasionally. (For example, Adam lived for 930 years = 186×5; Seth lived for 912 years = (181×5+7.) This could hardly be accidental and may indicate that the numbers are symbolic in some way which we fail to understand.

It is worth comparing the genealogies in Genesis with others from the ancient near east to see if we can learn something about how genealogies were used in the culture from which the Old Testament comes. There is a striking parallel to Genesis in what are called 'king lists' from ancient Sumeria, a culture which existed in southern Babylonia from about 3000 – 2300 BC. They date from well before the time of Abraham. The parallels between them and Genesis are set out below:

Sumerian king lists	*Genesis*
The creation of kingship	The creation of people
8 or 10 kings, each ruling between 43,000 – 18,600 years.	10 patriarchs, each living between 969 – 365 years.
The flood	The flood
More kings, each ruling between 1500 – 100 years.	More patriarchs, each living between 600 – 110 years.

The overall pattern is the same, though the biblical numbers are smaller than the Sumerian ones. To add to the parallels, in Sumerian tradition the seventh king was taken to heaven to have the secrets of the gods revealed to him. Compare this with Enoch, the seventh patriarch.

We shall return to this list when discussing the flood but the relevant point for us at the moment is that one of the later kings in the Sumerian list, En-Mebaragisi, is said to have reigned for 900 years. He is known from other evidence to have been a real person who lived for a quite normal time. Clearly the numbers here do not seem intended to be taken literally. Perhaps our problem is that 300 years of modern science have given us expectations regarding the use of numbers that are wrong when dealing with their use by the peoples of the ancient near east. Unfortunately we do not have any definite clues to help us understand the symbolic meaning of these large numbers in either the Sumerian or the biblical lists. Presumably the decrease in the lengths of reigns and lives symbolizes a decline of some kind in the human race. In Genesis this is, no doubt, primarily a moral decline.

CHAPTER 7
Events in Genesis 6–11

The story of Noah's flood is one of the best known Bible stories. As we shall see, there is no doubt that it was an historical catastrophe. The Bible makes it clear that the flood was an act of God's judgment on the human race because of its wickedness. Genesis 6:1–4 gives one example of that wickedness. Unfortunately the passage in which that comes is a very puzzling one:

> "1When men began to increase in number on the earth and daughters were born to them, 2the sons of God saw that the daughters of men were beautiful, and they married any of them they chose. 3Then the Lord said, "My Spirit will not contend with man for ever, for he is mortal; his days will be a hundred and twenty years."
>
> 4The Nephilim were on the earth in those days – and also afterwards – when the sons of God went to the daughters of men and had children by them. They were the heroes of old, men of renown.
>
> 5The Lord saw how great man's wickedness on the earth had become, and that every inclination of the thoughts of his heart was only evil all the time.

[6]The Lord was grieved that he had made man on the earth, and his heart was filled with pain. [7]So the Lord said, "I will wipe mankind, whom I have created, off from the face of the earth – men and animals, and creatures that move along the ground, and birds of the air – for I am grieved that I have made them."
[8]But Noah found favour in the eyes of the Lord.' (Genesis 6:1–8)

The sons of God

Who were these 'sons of God' who entered into marriages with the 'daughters of men' and so displeased God? At least three interpretations have received some support.

Fallen angels

Many take them to be fallen angels. The main support for this is that the usual meaning for the phrase 'sons of God' in the Old Testament is 'heavenly beings' (eg Job 1:6; Psalm 29:1). One objection to this interpretation is that it seems unfair of God to punish humans for an act instigated by fallen angels. A possible reply is that the women concerned and their fathers consented to these irregular unions, knowing that they were wrong.

Descendants of Seth

An almost equally popular view takes 'the sons of God' to be a reference to Seth's descendants. The list of Seth's descendants in Genesis 5 makes no mention of any sinful acts committed by them and includes the two exceptionally godly men, Enoch and Noah. Genesis 4:17–24 gives Cain's line. This includes Lamech, who committed bigamy and two vengeful murders. So, it is argued, the Sethites were more godly than the Cainites and therefore their marriages with Cainite women displeased God. The unusual use of the phrase 'the sons of God' which this requires is a major objection to this view. It may be justified by the fact that in Exodus 4:22 and elsewhere Israel is called God's 'son', and the Israelites are ultimately descended from Seth.

Ritual prostitution

A third, more recent and less well known interpretation sees the background to the story in the practice of ritual prostitution connected with many of the fertility cults of the ancient near east. In this case 'the sons of God' could refer to the priests or kings who were supposed to represent the pagan god in the sexual rites practised in the worship of the fertility gods. This is a plausible interpretation but, with such an unclear passage, one cannot be certain that it is right.

The difficult passage in 1 Peter 3:18–20, which refers to the disobedience before the flood can be interpreted to support any of these views.

Because none of the arguments for or against the different interpretations seems conclusive it would be wrong to insist that any one of them is *the* right one. All we can do is say which one seems to be the most likely.

The second interpretation seems the least likely. This is because it requires the unusual meaning of 'Sethite' for 'the sons of God' and because it is not at all clear from Genesis 4–5 that we are meant to see the Sethites as a whole as markedly more godly than the Cainites. The first interpretation has the merit of taking 'sons of God' in its most common Old Testament sense. However, since Genesis 1–11 is full of implicit attacks on the pagan religious practices and ideas of the ancient near east, I find the third interpretation the most likely.

The Nephilim

The Nephilim of 6:4 are mentioned only once elsewhere in the Bible: Numbers 13:33. There the Israelite spies meet them in Canaan and describe them as being of 'great size'. Some take the Nephilim to be the children of the irregular marriages. However, Genesis 6:4 does not actually say that but only that they existed at the time such marriages happened. This can be taken to imply that they existed before there were any such children. If they were the children of the marriages which displeased God it is surprising that they survived the flood which was partly a punishment for these marriages.

Words can change their meaning or have more than one meaning. The fact that the word 'Nephilim' only occurs twice, in stories relating to very different periods of time, means that we cannot be sure that it has the same meaning in both places. In either place it *could* refer to a distinct race of people but there is no fossil evidence of a distinct group of very tall people having existed in the near east at any time. This does not, however, mean that such a group did not exist, since the fossil evidence is very limited. Quite apart from this, however, it seems probable that 'Nephilim' was a term for people who were outstanding in some way, without implying that they were a special race on their own. In Numbers 13:33 the outstanding feature is size. The 'renown' in Genesis 6:4 probably refers to their quality as warriors, since that is a common meaning of the word which the NIV translates as 'heroes' in this verse.

The flood

Stories of a great flood are known from cultures around the world. J G Frazer quotes about 140 in his book *Folklore in the Old Testament*. We need to take care, though, in the significance we attach to this. There is reason to believe that some of the stories that have been collected are in fact retellings of the biblical story, first heard from missionaries. Secondly, many of them are widely different in detail from the biblical story and could have their origin in some quite different flood experience. After all, major floods do occur in many places from time to time. We will look at two aspects of the flood – its historicity and its universality – and at some of the practical details that are mentioned in the Genesis account.

An historical flood?

There is one set of flood stories so similar to the

biblical one that it is generally agreed that they originated in the same historical event. These are the flood stories from Mesopotamia. The best preserved of them is part of a long Babylonian poem called *The Gilgamesh Epic.* An earlier version of the story is found in another poem from Babylonia called *The Atrahasis Epic.* Both of these are known to have existed by about 1600 BC. A much earlier and fragmentary Sumerian account of the flood has also survived. In both *The Atrahasis Epic* and the Sumerian account there is an account of the creation of human beings followed by various divine judgments, culminating in the flood. This parallels the pattern of events in Genesis 1–9.

The main similarities between the Mesopotamian and biblical stories are these:

- After the multiplication of mankind a divine decision is taken to send a punishing flood to destroy them.
- One man is told to save himself, his family and some animals, by building a boat.
- A great flood destroys the rest of mankind.
- The boat grounds on a mountain in southern Armenia.
- Three times birds are sent out to determine when the land is habitable.
- The hero offers a sacrifice and is given a divine blessing.

There are also many differences between the Mesopotamian and biblical stories. The most obvious is that the Mesopotamian one assumes the existence of many gods, with Enlil as the chief god. More detailed differences are:

- Enlil wants to destroy mankind because their noisiness disturbs him, not because of their sinfulness.

• Contrary to the will of Enlil and the other gods a god called Enki warns one of his devoted worshippers to build a boat to escape the coming flood.

• The hero does not warn other people, but hides the reason for his boat-building from them.

• The size and shape of the boat, the passengers, and the duration of the flood all differ from the biblical story.

• The birds sent out are: a dove, a swallow, and a raven.

• The divine blessing is immortality for the hero and his wife.

Most of these differences have to do with the understanding of the significance of the flood and we will look at them in the next chapter. Others might have arisen as a result of changes as the story was constantly re-told. It is unlikely that the biblical story is based directly on one of the existing Mesopotamian versions, or vice versa. Most likely both they and the biblical story share a common source.

We saw in the last chapter that the Sumerian King Lists also mention the flood as a major disruption in history. Unfortunately the strange use of numbers in those lists means that they give no help in dating the flood. Since Sumerian history is fairly well documented by inscriptions from 2600 BC onwards with no mention of the flood, it must have happened earlier than this, probably a good deal earlier.

A universal flood?

There is no doubt that until about a century ago

nearly everyone took the story of the flood to refer to a universal flood covering the whole earth. It was primarily the impact of scientific considerations which led people to think again and to re-examine the biblical account to see whether it really did have to be understood in this way. If we take the flood as being universal we need to think about three difficulties raised by scientific studies.

Firstly, there does not appear to be any evidence for a world-wide flood. In order for the Himalayas to be covered the water would have to have been nearly six miles or nine kilometers deep. We would expect such a flood to have left thick layers of sediment that geologists could not miss. They have not, however, found them.

Advocates of the 'flood geology' school, have, as we have seen, proposed that it is all the fossil-bearing rocks, and many others, that are the result of the flood. Most geologists, however, think that there are many rock formations, some bearing fossils, which just cannot be explained by 'flood geology'. This is a rather technical subject and those who want to follow it up should read the books by D A Young (who holds to an anti-evolutionary, age-day position) listed at the end of this book. They are written in fairly popular terms.

If the fossil-bearing rocks are taken to be evidence of a universal flood, it seems that the flood must be dated to about 400 million years ago. The shells of some shellfish and corals show annual growth rings, like trees. However, if these are examined under a microscope they can be seen to be made up of daily growth rings, which can be counted. This is true of some fossil shells and corals too. The interesting fact is that such fossils from what is called the Devonian Period show 400 daily rings per annual ring! This is because, as a result of friction caused by the daily tides, the earth's rotation is slowing down and the day is getting longer. (Modern atomic clocks can measure this very accurately, at present it amounts to an increase of 0.000015 seconds per day each year.) This means that there are now fewer days in a year than there used to be. Calculations show that there were 400 days in a year about 400 million years ago. This is also the date that radioactive dating gives for the Devonian Period. Clearly this means that Devonian rocks and their fossils, and all those that lie beneath them in the rock strata, cannot give evidence of a recent, universal flood.

The second question that must be addressed is, where did all the water for the flood come from? It would seem that, to cover the whole earth to the depth required, eight times as much water would be needed as there is now in all the oceans.

One explanation is that God could have created this water miraculously and removed it miraculously.

An alternative theory, favoured by some flood geologists, is that between creation and the flood there was a canopy of water vapour above the earth's atmosphere ('the waters above the expanse' mentioned in Genesis 1:7). At the time of the flood this collapsed to give torrential rain. But this solution gives rise to another problem. Water vapour, like all gases, may be light but it does weigh something. The amount required to flood the earth would raise the atmospheric pressure (the weight of the atmosphere) from its present fifteen pounds per square inch to nearly 1000 pounds per square inch. Everything now alive on the earth's surface would be squashed flat! It could be that the creatures alive then were able to live under that pressure but, even if that was the case, it is difficult to see how they could have coped with the rapid and great drop in pressure when the canopy collapsed. The effect on them would presumably be similar to that on deep sea divers who, working at just a few times atmospheric pressure, die if they come up too quickly. The gases dissolved in their blood bubble out of it like the gas from a fizzy drink when it is poured out.

As a final point in connection with the theory of the water canopy, it is worth considering whether the reference in Genesis to 'the waters above the expanse' may refer instead to ordinary rain clouds. Psalm 148:4 uses the same phrase in reference to clouds after the flood.

Thirdly, a literal reading of the flood story raises a further difficulty. Genesis 7:20 says that the mountains were covered by more than twenty feet of water: 'The waters rose and covered the mountains to a depth of more than twenty feet.' Presumably Noah knew this because he knew that the Ark floated with about twenty feet of it under the water. When the Ark ran aground on the seventeenth day of the seventh month (8:4) there would have been twenty feet or so of water covering the place where it rested. The dry land could not be seen until the first day of the tenth month (8:5). If it took two-and-a-half months for about twenty feet of water to drain way, how long would a depth of six miles take to drain away?

With problems like these it seems worth re-examining our understanding of what the Bible says about the flood.

A local flood?

One point worth thinking about is that we would expect a major, world-wide flood to cause major changes on the surface of the earth. However, the way the location of Eden is described suggests that the reader is expected to recognize the location of this pre-flood site. At least two of the four rivers did not disappear in the flood. Here there may be a hint that the flood was not universal.

'Land' or 'the earth'?

Supporters of the idea that the flood was a local catastrophe, not a universal one, argue that the language of the story has been misread. The Hebrew word translated 'earth' in the story (*'eretz*) does not mean the same thing as the English word. In three-quarters of its occurrences in the Old Testament it is better translated by the word 'land', meaning a particular place or area, rather than 'earth'. The context has to be the guide. Also, there is a special Hebrew word for the whole inhabitable earth (*tebel*), and it is not used in the flood story. Try reading Genesis 6–9 with the word 'land' replacing 'earth' and you will see the different impression you get (usually where the English has 'earth', the Hebrew has 'the earth/land').

All people or all known people?

Statements like 'I am going to put an end to all people' (6:13) might seem to demand a universal interpretation of the flood. However, it is a feature of Old Testament language to use such apparently all-embracing phrases when they are not meant literally. For example 'all the countries' of Genesis 41:57 could hardly include the Americas or China, nor can the claim in 1 Kings 18:10 that Ahab searched all the nations and kingdoms for Elijah be taken literally. Hebrew speech is full of such 'exaggeration to make a point', which is not intended to be taken literally. It is quite possible that the flood story uses such language throughout to stress the greatness of the catastrophe but without meaning it literally. At most it may mean that all the land and people known to Noah were inundated by the flood.

These arguments from the text of the Bible itself do no more than suggest that a local interpretation of the story is possible. Those who adopt such an interpretation do so because they are persuaded that the scientific arguments favour a local flood rather than a universal one.

The location of the flood area

If the flood was only local, where did it happen? Most of those who adopt the local view assume that it occurred in Mesopotamia. This is partly because the story is followed by events in Babylonia, in southern Mesopotamia (the Tower of Babel, Abraham's call). The main reason, though, is the existence of the Mesopotamian flood stories. These are clearly set in Babylonia.

However, it has also been pointed out that the natural reading of the Hebrew of Genesis 11:2 is that the survivors of the flood entered Babylonia *from the east*: 'As men moved from the east, they found a plain in Shinar [Babylonia] and settled there' (the translation of the NIV footnote). It is then suggested that the flood occurred in the upland plateaux to the north and east of Babylonia, near the possible site of the garden of Eden and the mountains of Ararat. There is evidence that the Sumerians migrated to southern Babylonia from elsewhere, probably from further north. They may have brought the flood story with them and gradually adapted its details to match their new homeland.

In view of the lack of geographical evidence in the biblical story, other than the mention of the mountains of Ararat to the north-east of Mesopotamia, all attempts to be definite about the location of a local flood must be speculative.

Even if the flood was local, it could still have destroyed all humans other than those in the Ark if, at that time, they still lived in a restricted area. This view is hard to evaluate since we cannot say much about the possible date of the flood. However, if we link Adam with Neolithic culture, that culture did spread out from eastern Turkey quite rapidly. This means that a flood to wipe out all human beings would have to have happened fairly soon after the fall – a matter of a few hundred years later rather than thousands of years later.

From a purely numerical point of view there is nothing absurd in the suggestion that the present population of the earth might all be descended from eight people (Noah, his wife, his three sons and their wives) who lived about 3000–5000 BC. This would require the population to double every 150 to 200 years. It has been estimated that between 1630 and 1930 the earth's population doubled every 130 years.

The animals in the Ark

> '[19]You are to bring into the ark two of all living creatures, male and female, to keep them alive with you. [20]Two of every kind of bird, of every kind of animal and of every kind of creature that moves along the ground will come to you to be kept alive. [21]You are to take every kind of food that is to be eaten and store it away as food for you and for them.' (Genesis 6:19–21)

These verses raise a number of questions which are difficult to answer if the flood was universal. It is not a matter of what God *could* do, but what seems consistent with the way the story is told in Genesis, in which there is no indication of God doing a series of miracles to bring the animals to Noah, keep them alive on the Ark for just over a year and then disperse them all over the earth. For instance, how did the animals get from distant lands to the Ark? Unless the whole face of the earth was very different from what it is now, many would face insurmountable barriers such as major rivers, mountain ranges and oceans. How did they migrate home afterwards, when the earth was much as it is now? Once they were in the Ark the problems of feeding and caring for them would be enormous. Could just eight people feed, clean and generally look after tens of thousands of creatures?

Many more people are needed to run a large zoo today, which has far fewer animals! Very different living conditions would be needed by the various animals, some would need to be kept very cold while others would need it to be hot. Some would need to live in arid desert conditions while others would need to be cool and moist. How could this have been managed?

Of course, by miraculous intervention God could ensure that all these problems were solved – but the story gives no hint of him doing so.

These problems do not arise if the flood was only local; the number of animals involved would be very much fewer and the range of their needs less demanding. The language of the story would allow this, given what we have already seen of the tendency of Hebrew speech to 'exaggerate to make a point'.

A local or a universal flood? We have seen that the biblical account can be understood as referring to a local flood, that there is no clear geological evidence for a universal flood and that there are some strong scientific arguments against it. This leads me to the conclusion that the flood was a local catastrophe that occurred somewhere in the near east. The Sumerians knew of it, but it does not form part of the written records from Sumeria, which go back to about 3000 BC. This would indicate that the flood happened some time earlier than that.

The Tower of Babel

'[1]Now the whole world had one language and a
common speech. [2]As men moved eastward, they
found a plain in Shinar and settled there.
[3]They said to each other, "Come, let's make bricks
and bake them thoroughly." They used brick instead
of stone, and tar instead of mortar. [4]Then they said,
"Come let us build ourselves a city, with a tower
that reaches to the heavens, so that we may make a
name for ourselves and not be scattered over the face
of the whole earth."
[5]But the Lord came down to see the city and the
tower that the men were building. [6]The Lord said,
"If as one people speaking the same language they
have begun to do this, then nothing they plan to do
will be impossible for them. [7]Come, let us go down
and confuse their language so that they will not
understand each other."
[8]So the Lord scattered them from there over all
the earth, and they stopped building the city. [9]That
is why it was called Babel – because there the Lord
confused the language of the whole world. From
there the Lord scattered them over the face of the
whole earth.' (Genesis 11:1–9)

The purpose of the story

For anyone who is acquainted with Babylonian literature and religion Genesis 11:1–9 reads like a brilliant satire on the foundation of Babylon and its temples. No doubt this was what the author intended. It is interesting, and probably significant, that the Babylonian creation story *Enuma Elish* ends with the building of Babylon and the temple of Marduk, the chief god of Babylon and creator of the heavens and the earth.

In Akkadian, the language of Mesopotamia in Old Testament times, the name of Babylon is Babel. This means 'The Gate of Heaven'. The author of Genesis, however, links the name with the Hebrew verb meaning 'to confuse' (*bālal*). The most striking structure in ancient Babylon was a great stepped pyramid, called *Etemenanki*, 'The Temple Foundation of Heaven and Earth.' It was thought of as linking earth to heaven. The chief building in the temple enclosure was the temple of Marduk. This was called *Esagila*, 'The Temple that Raises its Head.' In the creation story its builders are said to have 'raised its head on high'.

The relevance of all this to the understanding of Genesis 11:1–9 is obvious. The writer is making fun of the claims of pagan religions to be the way to God. Instead of being an expression of human worship of God and the link between heaven and earth the temple tower is an expression of human pride and a form of rebellion against the true God. The 'Gate of Heaven' becomes the source of confusion and disunity among humans.

Historical significance

If this is the religious meaning of the story, what does it tell us historically? The answer to this depends on how the flood is understood. Those who believe that the flood, whether universal or local, destroyed all humans other than Noah's family, take this story to mark the beginning of the diversity of human languages and races.

In fact, the story does not necessarily claim this. Some argue that it describes what happened to one group of those who migrated from the area where the Ark came to rest, how they were dispersed and their language confused. It leaves open what happened to other groups. Three strands of evidence can be brought together to support this view.

Firstly, the genealogy in Genesis 10 describes the spread of Noah's descendants over the world known to the Israelites. Only one group of these, the sons of Cush, is linked with Babel and Mesopotamia (10:8–12). The genealogies in Genesis 4 and 5 cover the period from the fall to the flood. It seems reasonable, it is argued, to take the genealogy in Genesis 10 as covering a quite lengthy period between the flood and the Tower of Babel incident.

Secondly, it is also argued that the reference in verse 4 to the builders of the tower wanting to make a name for themselves and avoid being scattered implies that there were other people apart from them around. They wanted to be more famous than these people. Also, they feared that without a defensible city they might be attacked, defeated and scattered.

Thirdly, what about the references in the story to 'the whole earth'? Once again, as in the flood story, this could be translated as 'the whole land', meaning a large but limited area such as Mesopotamia. In historical times – that is, from the time that written records began – there has always been more than one language spoken in Mesopotamia at any one time. Genesis 11:1 can be taken as saying that there was once a time when only one language was spoken in the whole of that area. It is interesting that there is a Sumerian epic, *Enmerkar and the Lord Aratta*, which some scholars think tells of a time when people spoke only one language, which the chief god Enki changed into many languages. However, the text is fragmentary and not easy to understand.

Languages can be grouped into 'families' which have marked similarities in their vocabulary, grammar, the way they form words, and so on. For example, most of the languages spoken in Europe, Iran and north India belong to the 'Indo-European family' of languages. Middle-eastern languages such as Aramaic, Hebrew and Arabic belong to the 'Semitic family'. Individual languages within a 'family' probably developed as groups of people who originally all spoke the same language became separated geographically and developed their own special ways of speaking. The development of the Indo-European languages can be explained in this way. Linguistic experts are divided over whether or not there is evidence to suggest that the different 'families' have developed from an original single language. However, if the story of the Tower of Babel does refer to the founding of the famous city of Babylon we have to reckon with the fact that there is no evidence that Babylon existed earlier than about 2000 BC. We know that by then several different languages did exist. Of course, the story could refer to a much earlier, unsuccessful, attempt to found a city on the site of Babylon.

The evidence is so inconclusive that it seems best to suspend judgment and accept that, even if we believe in a universal destruction of humans by the flood, we should not insist that the Tower of Babel incident explains the origin of all languages. We should accept that it might refer to the origin of only one 'family' of languages. This 'localized' understanding of the Babel incident has to be adopted by those who believe that the flood destroyed only a part of the human race alive at that time.

CHAPTER 8
Get the Message?

It is inevitable that, as children of a scientific age, we want to relate what we read in Genesis 1–11 to the findings of science. It is tragic, though, if we do this at the expense of listening to what Genesis is trying to teach us. We do not need to resolve all the scientific disputes related to it before we can understand this. If we did, all those who have read the Bible without the benefit of modern scientific knowledge have been at a grave disadvantage! It would be surprising if God allowed that to be true of his word. Arguably, if we need any additional knowledge in order to understand Genesis, knowing something about the religions and cultures of the ancient near east is of more value than knowing something about science. It is easier to see what the author's main points are when they are highlighted by contrast with the beliefs he is opposing.

A detailed study of the message of these chapters would require writing another book. What follows will be only an outline sketch of that message.

Instead of going through it chapter-by-chapter we will look at a number of themes: the nature of God; the nature of the world; the problem of evil; what it means to be human; and God's plan of salvation.

What is God like?

Read against the background of Babylonian, Canaanite or Egyptian religious literature, especially their creation stories, the striking thing about Genesis 1–3 is its monotheism, its assumption that *there is only one God*. One form of the Babylonian creation epic begins with the birth of the gods from the waters of chaos. Marduk, the god of Babylon, gains his superior position by overcoming the forces of chaos and creating the world. In Genesis there is only ever one God, the creator. The 'us' of 1:26 ('Then God said, "Let us make man in our image, in our likeness" '), in no way contradicts this. It may be a royal 'we', or an address to the heavenly court of (non-divine) angels. It may prepare the way for the later trinitarian understanding of God, but it does not proclaim it.

We have seen in chapter 5 that the reference to the sun and moon as merely 'lights' is a rejection of the worship of the heavenly bodies as gods. Marduk of Babylon was the sun-god. If the traditional understanding of 1:1–2 is correct, then we are being told that *God existed alone before anything was created*. There are no primeval, eternal waters of chaos.

Mention of the waters of chaos leads to another aspect of God that is very clear in Genesis 1 in particular – *his sovereign power*. He does not have to do battle with the forces of chaos before creating the world. We have seen that using the special verb 'to create' (*bara'*) in reference to the creation of the sea monsters (1:21) is an attack on any such idea. God simply speaks and his will is done.

The wisdom of God is displayed in the order and pattern of his work of creation. Proverbs 8:22–31 and Isaiah 40:12–14 take up this theme.

The flood story in Genesis shows *the grace of God*, in striking contrast to the Babylonian story. In the Babylonian story it is only the fact that one of the gods breaks the promise, made by all the gods, not to warn humans of the flood that leads to a few escaping it. In Genesis it is an act of grace on the part of God to warn Noah.

Comparison of the Genesis story with the Babylonian version brings out another aspect of God, *his moral nature*. In Genesis the flood is clearly an act of judgment on human sinfulness. It is an act of justice, not of selfish pique or revenge. In the Babylonian version the flood is sent for a quite non-moral reason. Enlil gets irritated and touchy because the humans are so noisy that they disturb his sleep!

So then, Genesis 1–11 presents us with the claim that there is one true God, the creator, who is sovereign over the world. He acts wisely and justly. His justice is seasoned with grace.

What is the world like?

The most obvious thing about the world in Genesis is that it is *a created world*. It owes its existence and character to God and so is dependent on him. This is spelt out more fully in the New Testament (Colossians 1:15–17; Hebrews 1:1–4).

Genesis 1 stresses that, as originally created, *the world was 'good'*. The meaning of its goodness is clear from the context – it pleased God. It pleased him because it reflected something of himself. One aspect of this was its order and harmony, which is emphasized in the careful structure of the creation account. Such order and harmony is a large part of what is meant by the Hebrew word *shalôm*. This is often translated into English as 'peace', but means not so much the *absence* of conflict or other forms of disturbance as the *presence* of the kind of order and harmony that allows people to live life as God wants it lived. The fact that the creation pleased God also means that it was free of evil, which becomes the major cause of the absence of *shalôm* after the fall.

In some religions the material world is thought to be intrinsically evil. Some forms of Greek philosophy taught this, in particular the very influential philosophy of Plato. Basically, all that is 'material' rather than 'spiritual' was seen as 'evil'. The early Christian theologians realized that such a view of the material world is unbiblical. But Greek ideas had such a big impact on western thought that some strands of Christianity are still suspicious of material things and bodily pleasures. Of course these things can be used in a sinful way but God's creation is essentially good; it is not wrong to enjoy it as long as we do so in obedience to his law.

Because the world is God's good creation, we should respect it and make use of it responsibly. We are not to despoil and deface it. We shall return to this theme later.

Evil

The goodness of the original creation brings us to the problem of evil. Genesis does not explain the ultimate origin of evil. The serpent is introduced without explanation of how it came to be opposed to God. However, two things are made clear. Firstly, *evil is not something co-equal or co-eternal with God*. The serpent is not another God but a perverted creature. Secondly, as we have seen, evil is not part of the original nature of creation. Part of God's creation (including Adam and Eve) was given the opportunity and ability to choose to rebel against him, and did so. Evil is a distortion of God's good creation. In essence it is the rebellion of the creature against its creator. That being so, there is hope. Surely the sovereign creator is able to overcome the rebellion and remove the distortion in his own time and way!

This view of evil stands in marked contrast to what is found in some other religions. Some do make evil co-equal and co-eternal with God or the gods. This seems to have been the case with the religions of Mesopotamia and Canaan, which attributed what we would call 'evil' to the acts of the gods themselves. Some of the gods were seen as essentially evil – the bringers of famine, plague and so on. Other religions, like Platonism, see evil as eternal and an essential part of the material world. These are pessimistic views, because they imply that there can be no ultimate removal of evil and triumph of good. Some of the eastern religions and New Age philosophies that are gaining popularity in the West today regard evil as ultimately an illusion, a result of our frustrated desires. If we can learn to live free from desire we will realize that neither good nor evil exists. Most of us would think that an unrealistic view. The Bible is thoroughly realistic. Evil is real and God hates it. It devastates his world. But the Bible is also optimistic in the long run. God is at work dealing with evil and one day will remove it completely.

Human nature

The Babylonian creation accounts agree with Genesis that humans are different from other creatures. We are *a mixture of the earthly and the heavenly*. In the *Atrahasis Epic* one of the gods is killed and his blood is mixed with clay to create humans. According to Genesis 1–3 we are on one level no different from the animals, made out of the dust of the earth. It is therefore not surprising that there is little difference between the basic biochemistry of the cells that make up our bodies and the cells of other animals, even the humble yeast cell. Nor should we be disturbed by the fact that we have other resemblances to the animals – in our instincts, behaviour patterns and so on.

Where some people go wrong is to assume that this animal-likeness is *all* that there is to be said about humans. This assumption often arises because of a failure to recognize the limitations of science. Genesis teaches, and our experience bears it out, that there is another level or aspect to human nature. This is our spiritual nature. We alone of the created beings are said to *bear God's image and likeness* (1:26–27). What does this mean? Scholars have debated this question long and often and are not fully agreed as to the exact answer. Some have tried to make a distinction between 'image' and 'likeness'. This is probably not valid; in Genesis 5:1–3 the two terms seem to be used interchangeably. Also, the doubling up of similar terms like this is a common feature of Hebrew literature. It is generally agreed that attempts to define the 'image' in terms of one particular human quality (eg reason, moral sense, love) are mistaken. It is wider than that. We do best to think of it in terms of being made in such a way that we can reflect something of God's nature in our personality. The fact that we are made in this way prepares for the amazing event of the coming of Christ – of God the Son becoming a man. He was the perfect human image of God (2 Corinthians 4:4; Colossians 1:15).

Because we bear the image of God we are *God's representatives on earth*, and are given the authority to rule it on his behalf (Genesis 1:26–28). The point is sometimes made that in the ancient near east a conqueror of a city would usually leave behind a statue of himself, sometimes with his laws inscribed on it, as a reminder of his authority over that city when he left it and went back home. In the light of that, we can speak of humans as the symbols of God's rule and authority over the earth. Perhaps one reason for the prohibition in the ten commandments against making images of God is that this not only limits and distorts our view of God but it forgets that humans are the only images of God allowed on earth! This is a very different valuation of humans than that of the Babylonians. Their creation stories say that we were created to be the slaves of the gods, providing them with their food and drink (through sacrifices) and building houses (temples) for them.

All views which see people as a means to an end, rather than as of value in themselves, fall short of the biblical valuation of human beings. This could be said of some modern political ideologies, such as Fascism and Marxism, which tend to treat the ordinary person simply as a means to achieving a political Utopia.

Humans were created by God *as sexual beings*, as men and women. In Genesis 1:27 the creation of humans as 'male and female' is closely related to the image of God. Since God is not a physical being it cannot be the case that we reflect him simply in our sexuality. We may, however, have here a hint of the 'communal' nature of God which is represented in the doctrine of the trinity. God's 'personality' is of a different, more complex, order than ours. It is better represented by the picture (image) of humans living together in loving, harmonious relationship than by that of an isolated individual human personality. In saying this we must remember what was said in chapter 2 about doctrines as models or pictures, and not take the picture literally.

Genesis 2:18–24 says more about our sexuality than does Genesis 1:26–27. Because of the tendency to regard bodily desires as evil, some Christians have had a negative view of sex, especially its physical expression. But here we are clearly told that sex was God's idea! He thought it good that there should be men and women and that they should 'become one flesh', the biblical expression for sexual intercourse. But, and this is very important, the creator of sex has also told us the right way in which it should be expressed and enjoyed. This is within the relationship of lifelong, single-partner marriage with a member of the opposite sex. This is the clear teaching of Genesis 2:24, to which Jesus appealed in his teaching (Mark 10:6–9): 'For this reason a man will leave his father and mother and be united to his wife, and they will become one flesh.'

Genesis 2:18 is sometimes, wrongly, taken to imply that women are inferior to men, simply their 'helpers': 'The Lord God said, "It is not good for the man to be alone. I will make a helper suitable for him." ' In fact the Hebrew word used here (*'ezer*) is most often used of God when he helps his people (eg 1 Samuel 7:12). It hardly implies inferiority! On the contrary, woman is described as a suitable partner for man in the task of caring for God's world. *Men and women are different, but truly complementary* in that they 'complete' one another, the one making up for what the other lacks. The essential equality of men and women is beautifully expressed in the story of Eve's creation, whether or not we take it literally. It speaks of woman being made of the same substance as man. Unlike the animals, she is not made out of a separate dust heap but from Adam's own body. It is probably significant that she is made from his rib. As it has been said: not from his head, to rule over him, or from his feet to be trodden on by him but from his side to be his equal.

As we have seen, Genesis 1:26–28 gives to men and women the authority to 'subdue' and 'rule' the world. Some have seen this as a charter for the selfish exploitation of the earth. However, this authority must be seen in the context of men and women bearing God's image. We are expected to rule the world in God's place, as he would rule it. This means that we will not want to despoil what he saw as 'very good' when he had completed it. Our treatment of the world should reflect his wisdom and justice in the way we develop its resources and share them out among ourselves.

Finally, Genesis teaches that *we are worshipping beings*. This is shown by God blessing the seventh day and making it holy. We are made to live in a loving relationship with our creator and need to put aside time to develop this through prayer, meditation on God's word and worship. To some extent this is to be done individually but, because we are social creatures, it is also to be done in fellowship with other people. In his wisdom God gave us the pattern of setting aside one day in seven to rest from work and the other concerns that take up much of our time and to spend time deepening our relationship with him.

Augustine of Hippo expressed the need that we have for a relationship with God when he said, 'Lord you made us for yourself, and we are restless until we find our rest in you.' When people ignore or reject God, that restlessness leads them to worship other 'gods', such as money, pleasure and power.

Fallen human nature

It is right that creatures should recognize and respect their creator. But God wants such recognition and respect to be given freely by men and women. This is why he gave Adam and Eve the test he did regarding the tree of the knowledge of good and evil. He gave them the opportunity to decide whether nor not to live in obedience to him.

It is not absolutely clear what that tree represents. Some limit it to moral knowledge but a Hebrew phrase like this, stating two opposites, can be taken to mean 'everything'. Perhaps the right way to understand the test is to see it as meaning that the human search for knowledge of all kinds should be carried out in dependence on God and in the light of his revelation. We are not to grab knowledge purely for our own selfish ends.

Whatever the exact nature of the test, Adam and Eve failed. They gave in to the temptation to be like God in a wrong sense, to be his rivals instead of his representatives, and so became sinners. The effects of that sin is pictured in what follows. It can be seen in terms of four disrupted relationships.

- Most importantly, the relationship between us and our creator has been affected. Instead of free and intimate friendship, there is fear and a shrinking from his presence (3:8–10).
- We are no longer at peace with ourselves. We have a sense of unease and shame (2:25; 3:7).
- We can no longer get on with each other. We start blaming other people for what goes wrong (3:12). What should have been the deepest and happiest relationship becomes a place of strife and exploitation. (3:16).
- Our relationship with nature becomes a source of frustration, so that we seem always to be battling with it (3:17–19).

Here in this simple story is a powerful presentation of the spiritual source of our psychological, social, and environmental problems. They all flow from the loss of a right relationship with our creator God.

In Genesis 4–6 we see the effects of sin spreading out like the ripples from a stone thrown into a pond. The murderous jealousy of Cain, the vengefulness of Lamech and the sexual immorality of 'the sons of God', build up to the widespread evil in the generation of Noah. At that point God steps in to demonstrate that he will not tolerate the uninhibited spread of evil.

Yet in this dark picture there are chinks of light. We are told that the image of God has not been removed from humans. Adam and Eve pass it on to their children (5:1–3). The image may be marred and distorted, but it is not totally destroyed. It is still possible to live in a right relationship with

God, as Enoch did (5:21–24). Had the image been lost completely we would not be human any more but simply complex animals. The fact that we remain in God's image gives us some ground for hope. God has not given up on his purpose for his creation.

Salvation

This brings us to the subject of God's plan of salvation. Alongside each of God's acts of punishment of sin in Genesis 1–11 goes a gracious act of mercy. This is most obvious in the case of the flood. In this case, not only does God save Noah and his family but, at the end of the flood, he makes a covenant with all creation not to carry out a similar widespread punishment of sin whilst this world-order remains. It is there also in the case of Cain. He is doomed to be a restless wanderer but in answer to his own plea he is given a mark to protect his life. Similarly, when Adam and Eve are driven out of Eden, God himself clothes them. Here we have hints that it is not God's intention to wipe out his creation that has fallen into sin, but to limit the effects of that sin and maybe to do more than that. But how will he do it?

Genesis 1–11 is the prologue to the Bible, so it does not answer that question fully but it indicates where the answer will lie. When the serpent is cursed there is a promise that the offspring of the woman will one day crush the head of the serpent – that is, destroy the source of evil (3:15). How this will come about begins to unfold after the incident of the Tower of Babel. At first this seems to be the one act of punishment for sin in Genesis 1–11 which lacks any corresponding act of grace. This is because the act of grace is actually recorded in Genesis 12:1–3. At Babel humankind was confused and scattered by God. Now we are told of how God called a man to become the father of a nation through which all the scattered nations would be blessed.

So the story that leads through the great men and women of faith to Jesus the Saviour begins to unfold and, through him to the new heaven and the new earth, where the redeemed of humanity from every nation and language group live once again in the immediate presence of God and have access to the tree of life.

CHAPTER 9
Genesis and Science Today

As we have looked at ideas about the relationship of science to Genesis you may have been surprised by the variety of views and lack of conclusive answers. You should not be. Our understanding of anything, including the Bible, is never perfect. What is more, as we saw in chapter 2, science is always only an approximation to ultimate reality. If our interpretation of the Bible agreed perfectly with the modern science of today, it almost certainly would not agree with the modern science of tomorrow! The really important thing is that we should understand exactly what Genesis teaches.

In the opening chapters of this book we saw that science provides only one, limited, way of looking at the world – in terms of its *mechanism*. Christianity, we argued, provides a different but complementary view – concerned with the *meaning* of life in this world. We would expect the Bible, the source-book of Christian teaching, to be primarily concerned with questions of meaning rather than mechanism. This turns out to be the case for Genesis 1–11, especially if we read these chapters according to the literary-cultural approach, which seems to me to be the right approach. For example, we saw that although Genesis 1–3 teaches that God created human beings it does not rule out the possibility that he did so through an evolutionary process. Whether he did or not is a question which it is proper for science to investigate.

Although the Bible leaves very many questions like this wide open for scientific study, there are two ways in which it sometimes comes into direct contact with science.

Revelation and history

In the Bible God reveals to us the spiritual truth he wants us to know. Some of that revelation comes through accounts of things that God has done in the course of world history. It is right and proper for us to ask whether historians and scientists can find any evidence concerning these events or throw any other light on them – and to take seriously the answers they give as another way of discovering the truth which ultimately has its source in God. We asked these kinds of questions about the flood. The historical and scientific evidence suggested that it was a major catastrophe in the history of the near east but was probably not a world-wide one. Such an understanding of it does not conflict with the way the story is told in Genesis 6–9. If it did, we would have to ask the historians and scientists to re-examine their conclusions or look for more evidence because we would expect that ultimately their conclusions would be compatible with the biblical account.

When appealing to scientific and historical evidence we have to be careful, for two reasons. The first is the nature of biblical language. If it is symbolic language, or some other kind of figurative language, it may not be easy to relate what is said to scientific or historical evidence. Secondly, God is free to do miracles which do not fit into the normal course of history or the laws of nature. However, it is unwise to appeal to miracles to explain things – as some do, for example, with aspects of the flood – when the Bible does not speak of God doing miracles.

A way of seeing things

In chapter 2 the Christian way of understanding reality was compared to an artist's impression of a building and the scientific view was compared to one of the architect's plans. This indicates another, more far-reaching, way in which the Bible can interact with science. For the Christian scientific truth has to be seen within the framework provided by the distinctive view of reality which results from accepting the teaching of the Bible.

Genesis 1–11 is a very important section of the Bible because these chapters contribute a great deal to the formation of an overall view of reality. We have seen what these chapters teach about such fundamental matters as the nature of God, the nature of the world, what it means to be human, evil and salvation. All of this has implications which the Christian must take seriously in relation to science.

Science, God and creation

Genesis 1 teaches that we live in a universe created by God. Science can neither prove nor disprove this. At most scientists may be able to tell us the processes which God used to bring into being the universe as we know it. Even if it is true that the universe developed from a 'quantum vacuum' according to well-known physical laws, that does not make God unnecessary. We are still left asking, 'Why should there be a quantum vacuum with the potential to produce a universe?' The unbeliever may reply that it is just 'the way things are'. It is at least as rational to reply that there is a God who created the quantum vacuum and that the physical laws are God at work shaping his creation. In chapter 1 we saw that it was this Christian view of the universe which formed the basis of modern science and that, without it, it is difficult to find a rational basis for science.

Science and people

We have seen that Genesis teaches that we are made out of the dust of the ground but also made in the image of God. We are both earthly and heavenly, material and spiritual. Being bearers of God's image sets us apart from the animals but being made out of the dust of the ground unites us with them.

It is right that in their quest to understand people

better, scientists should sometimes study the human brain as if it were a computer or compare human behaviour with that of animals. However, Christians must protest when some then claim that we are *just* machines with no freewill, or *nothing but* complex animals. Such claims are contradicted by biblical teaching. They are also logically invalid because they take one, limited, view of reality as the total picture. Scientists adopt such limited views as a way of isolating one aspect of a complicated thing (in this case a person) so that they can have something simple enough to study. But what is learnt in this way must then be fitted back into the bigger picture, not taken to be the whole picture. We want to say that Christian teaching sketches out an outline of that picture, which is then filled in with the help of knowledge from other sources.

Science and technology

According to Genesis 1–2 God gave humans *the responsibility of caring for his creation* and *the right to make use of it to meet their needs.* Belief in this responsibility and this right was one of the things which motivated the early scientists to study the world and develop technologies to make use of their discoveries for the benefit of the human race.

We have to face the fact that things have often gone wrong, sometimes terribly so. The right to use the world has been separated from the responsibility to care for it as God would have done. What was originally very good has been defaced and despoiled. This is, of course, a result of greed and selfishness – expressions of the fallenness of human nature. Christians should be in the forefront of those who protest at the damage being done to our environment, God's good creation, by the thoughtless or wrongly exploitive use of science and technology. We should be pressing for technology to be used in ways that are environmentally sound. Any unavoidable environmental damage should be counted as part of the cost of the technology and should be repaired as far as possible out of its profits.

Scientists: finite and fallen

Scientists are human beings. Like all of us they are both finite and fallen. Their finiteness means that their understanding of the universe is always incomplete. As a result it is sometimes mistaken because some vital aspect of the truth is missing.

Because they are fallen their attitudes, motives and methods are sometimes wrong. Instead of seeking the truth for its own sake a scientist may be more interested in his or her reputation. As a result there may be a refusal to face up to evidence which challenges a pet theory, or even, in extreme cases, a falsification of results so that they fit the theory. A desire to get results at all costs may lead to a refusal to stop and ask awkward questions about the experimental methods being used, and an impatience with those who do – for example, 'Should animals be used in experiments and, if so, under what circumstances?' 'Should experiments be carried out on tissue from aborted foetuses?'

The fallenness of men and women means that

the powers which science and technology make available to us are sometimes used in harmful ways. The knowledge and skills which lead to genetically engineered bacteria which produce insulin to help diabetics can also be used to produce bacteria for germ warfare. Here is a challenge for scientists to get together with ethicists and other representatives of society to find ways of controlling the use of scientific discoveries and skills.

Science and salvation

Of course the picture is not all black. Far from it! Science and technology have done a great deal to benefit the human race but there is now a more balanced assessment of their achievements than was the case thirty or forty years ago.

Earlier this century many thought and hoped that by education (especially in science), social welfare programmes (in which such sciences as medicine and nutrition would play a big part) and technology the human race would finally reach a reasonable approximation to the ideal society – in a sense achieve its own 'salvation'. World wars (made more horrific by chemical and atomic weapons), corrupt politicians and bureaucrats and the environmental damage caused by some technologics have dashed those hopes.

The Bible teaches that the only real way of salvation is to be found in accepting the good news of what God has done for us through Jesus Christ. His death and resurrection make it possible for us to receive God's forgiveness and the power of his Spirit. That power gradually restores his image in our personality, undoing the ravages of the fall. But the good news is not just about individual salvation. The restoration of our relationship with God and the image of God in us enables us to work at the restoration of the other relationships damaged by the fall – our social relationships and our relationship with nature – so as to make them as pleasing to God as we can.

This is *not* a matter of trying to achieve utopia, heaven on earth, by our own efforts. It *is* a matter of joining battle with God against the evil that has entered his creation and despoiled it. The knowledge and power that science gives us can be used to aid us in this battle. But if it is to be used in this way it has to be understood within the framework of the Christian view of reality. As we have seen, Genesis 1–11, properly interpreted and understood, makes a major contribution to the formation of that view.

The most important things to gain from this book are not answers to the historical or scientific problems raised by Genesis 1–11. Those answers do have some value in helping us come to a better understanding of these chapters and a deeper confidence in them. However, it is more important to understand the message of these chapters and to let them shape our understanding of life. That will then help us to live in the way that God wants us to, as people made in his image and likeness.

Further reading

The following list contains the books referred to in *Genesis Today*, together with some books for those who want to read further on the subjects covered.

P Atkins, *The Creation*. Oxford: W H Freeman, 1981.

R J Berry, *God and Evolution*. London: Hodder and Stoughton, 1988. Advocates a theistic evolutionary position.

H Blocher, *In the Beginning*. Leicester: IVP, 1984. An outstanding study of Genesis 1–3. Concerned primarily with the meaning of the text.

J Calvin, *Institutes of the Christian Religion*. Philadelphia: Westminster Press, 1960.

A C Custance, *The Flood: Local or Global?* Grand Rapids: Zondervan, 1979. Argues for a local flood.

R Dawkins, *The Blind Watch-Maker*. Harmondsworth: Penguin, 1988.

J G Frazer, *Folklore in the Old Testament*. London: Macmillan, 1919. A classic collection which needs to be used with care.

J B S Haldane, *Possible Worlds*. London: Chatto and Windus, 1932.

A Hayward, *Creation and Evolution: Facts and Fallacies*. London: SPCK, 1985. Argues for an anti-evolutionary version of the 'Age-day' approach.

A Heidel, *The Gilgamesh Epic and Old Testament Parallels*. Chicago: University of Chicago Press, 1963.

A Heidel, *The Babylonian Genesis*. Chicago: University of Chicago Press, 1963.

F Hoyle and N Wickramasinghe, *Evolution From Space*. London: Dent, 1981.

S Jaki, *Science and Creation*. Edinburgh: Scottish Academic Press, 1974. A detailed study of the rise of modern science.

W G Lambert and A R Millard, *Atrahasis*. Oxford: Clarendon Press, 1969.

D N Livingstone, *Darwin's Forgotten Defenders*. Edinburgh: Scottish Academic Press, 1987. An interesting study of evangelical reactions to Darwin.

J MacMurray, *Reason and Emotion*. London: Faber and Faber, 1962.

J Monod, *Chance and Necessity*. London: Collins, 1983.

H M Morris, *Scientific Creationism*. Edinburgh: Christian World Publishers, 1974. A young earth, flood geology approach.

J Orr, *The Christian View of God and the World*. Edinburgh: Andrew Elliot, 1904.

E K V Pearce, *Who was Adam?* Exeter: Paternoster, 1969. An interesting variant of theistic evolution.

M W Poole and G J Wenham, *Creation or Evolution – A False Antithesis?* Oxford: Latimer House, 1987.

B Ramm, *The Christian View of Science and Scripture*. Exeter: Paternoster, 1964. Favours the 'revelatory day' approach to Genesis 1, and a local flood.

M Ridley, *The Problems of Evolution*. Oxford: Oxford University Press, 1985. A scientific defence of evolution.

C A Russell, *Cross-Currents*. Leicester: IVP, 1985. A very readable account of the history of science.

J P Sartre, *Existentialism and Humanism*. London: Methuen, 1973.

D Spanner, *Biblical Creation and the Theory of Evolution*. Exeter: Paternoster, 1987. Argues that evolution is compatible with the biblical teaching on creation.

G J Wenham, *Genesis 1–15*. Waco: Word Books, 1987. A very valuable scholarly commentary.

J C Whitcomb and H M Morris, *The Genesis Flood*. Grand Rapids: Baker, 1961. The classic statement of 'young earth, flood geology' position.

P J Wiseman, *Clues to Creation in Genesis*. London: Marshall, Morgan Scott, 1977. Argues for a 'revelatory day' interpretation of Genesis 1.

D A Young, *Creation and the Flood*. Grand Rapids: Baker, 1977. Argues for an anti-evolution, 'Age-day' position.

D A Young, *Christianity and the Age of the Earth*. Grand Rapids: Zondervan, 1982. Takes an anti-evolution, 'Age-day' position.